Traeger Grill
Book for Beginners

Tasty & Easy Traeger Recipes for Outdoor Cooking & BBQ Enthusiasts | Step-by-Step
Cooking Instructions to Help You Create Perfect Wood Fire Flavored Meals

Beatrice Chastain

Table of Contents

1   **Introduction**

2   **Fundamentals of Traeger Wood Fire Grills**

11   **4-Week Meal Plan**

13   **Chapter 1 Breakfast Recipes**

21   **Chapter 2 Vegetables and Sides Recipes**

34   **Chapter 3 Poultry Recipes**

49   **Chapter 4 Beef Recipes**

62   **Chapter 5 Pork Recipes**

73   **Chapter 6 Lamb and Venison Recipes**

83   **Chapter 7 Fish and Seafood Recipes**

95   **Conclusion**

96   **Appendix 1 Measurement Conversion Chart**

97   **Appendix 2 Recipes Index**

Introduction

The Traeger pellet grill is one of the top-selling products on the market today. While many people are familiar with it, others may not have heard of it before. This guide provides comprehensive information about the Traeger pellet grill, helping you understand its benefits and determine if it's suitable for you, your home, and your business. By the end, you might prefer the Traeger grill over traditional charcoal and gas grills.

Pellet grills are outdoor cookers that use advanced technology to ignite all-natural hardwood pellets as a fuel source for heating and cooking food. They are electric-powered and automated, ensuring precise cooking with a delicious wood-fired flavor.

Using a pellet grill allows you to cook with a cleaner-burning fuel source, which is both safe and efficient. Unlike traditional charcoal or propane grills, pellet grills do not produce strong, harsh smoke and gas odors. They offer an easy and relaxing outdoor cooking experience, providing many years of enjoyment.

If you live in a small to medium-sized area with limited backyard space, the Traeger pellet grill is an excellent option. It eliminates the need for a bulky charcoal grate and ensures a pleasant grilling experience. Perfect for grilling fish, meat, kabobs, steaks, and chicken, the Traeger grill is designed to make outdoor cooking straightforward and enjoyable.

The Traeger grill is portable, allowing you to take it with you on various occasions. It delivers excellent performance, cooking meat, fish, vegetables, and more to perfection. Tested by numerous users, the Traeger grill consistently outperforms other brands on the market, providing a superior grilling experience.

In summary, the Traeger pellet grill is a top-rated product that offers convenience, efficiency, and exceptional cooking results, making it a great addition to your outdoor cooking equipment.

If you are new to grilling and unsure how to use it, it can feel overwhelming at first. But don't worry, I'm here to guide you every step of the way, and it can truly transform your lifestyle. The Traeger grill is simple and very user-friendly. Soon, you'll be cooking various recipes on the grill grate and impressing your friends and family. Try my recipes and read all the guidance about this appliance.

Fundamentals of Traeger Wood Fire Grills

There are many reasons why we love grilling, such as reducing fat, creating an instant party atmosphere, using less sauce, and its many other benefits. Since we are talking about the best grill, the Traeger wood pellet grill, we will take you through a wealth of information about this product. Through our introduction, you will not only learn about its excellent performance but also pick up a thing or two about its unique features.

The Traeger wood pellet grill is not just a cooking tool; it is an essential device that enhances your grilling experience. Whether you aim to reduce fat intake for a healthier diet or to enjoy the fun of outdoor gatherings, this grill can meet your needs. Its design not only minimizes the use of sauces, preserving the natural flavor of ingredients but also offers various cooking methods to diversify your recipes.

Next, we will provide a detailed introduction to the functions and advantages of the Traeger wood pellet grill, giving you a comprehensive understanding of why it is one of the most popular grills on the market. You will learn how to utilize its unique design and technology to achieve perfect grilling results and truly enjoy the pleasures of barbecuing.

What Is Traeger Wood Fire Grills?

The Traeger wood pellet grill combines the features of a charcoal grill and an oven, allowing you to cook food over an open flame. On cold days, you can turn on your Traeger grill to enjoy a variety of foods. It operates by using a motor that moves a screw, which controls the pellet fire to increase or decrease the flame. The smoke and flames are directed into the chimney, reducing the risk of hazards and preventing meat from burning.

The use of wood adds an extra level of flavor, enhancing the taste of your dishes. Traeger grills use hardwood pellets available in various flavors, such as Alder, Oak, Hickory, Apple, Cherry, Maple, Mesquite, and Pecan.

How Does It Work?

A Traeger grill uses hardwood pellets that come in various flavors, such as Alder, Hickory, Oak, Apple, Maple, Cherry, Mesquite, and Pecan. To begin, fill the hopper with the pellet flavor of your choice. When you turn on the grill using the controller, an auger moves the pellets from the hopper to the firepot.

Once in the firepot, the pellets are ignited by the ignition rod, and smoke begins to roll. This smoke

infuses your food with a delicious and unique smoky flavor. A conduction fan circulates the smoke and heat, ensuring even distribution and resulting in tender and flavorful food. You can easily adjust the temperature to match your recipe's instructions using a straightforward dial.

When the grill reaches the desired temperature, place your food onto the grill grate. The drip pan beneath the grill grate serves multiple purposes, including catching juices and grease that drip from the food as it cooks, preventing flare-ups and keeping the cooking area clean.

Additionally, you can download an app on your smartphone to monitor both the grill and food temperatures from anywhere in your home. The app allows you to control the grill's temperature with precision, ensuring stunning results for your dishes. This method of cooking is incredibly convenient, allowing you to enjoy time with your family while keeping an eye on your food through your phone. The Traeger grill makes it easy to cook delicious meals at home without spending long hours in the kitchen.

Benefits of Using Traeger Wood Fire Grills

1.Versatility:
The Traeger grill can smoke, grill, bake, roast, braise, and BBQ, allowing you to prepare a wide range of dishes from savory meats and vegetables to tasty pizzas and desserts.

2.Consistent Temperature Control:
The digital temperature control system maintains precise heat levels, ensuring consistent cooking results and eliminating the need for constant monitoring.

3.Enhanced Flavor:
Cooking with hardwood pellets infuses your food with a rich, smoky flavor that is hard to achieve with traditional gas or charcoal grills.

4.Healthier Cooking:
Using wood pellets as a fuel source results in cleaner combustion, producing less harmful emissions compared to charcoal or gas grills. Additionally, the even heat distribution helps reduce the need for excess oils and fats.

5.Ease of Use:
The automated system with digital controls makes the Traeger grill user-friendly. Simply set your desired temperature, and the grill takes care of the rest.

6.Low Maintenance:
Traeger grills are designed for easy cleaning and maintenance. The grease management system and the use of hardwood pellets produce less ash and residue.

7.Convenience:
The Traeger grill's ability to maintain consistent temperatures and cook food evenly means you can set it and forget it, freeing you up to enjoy your time with family and friends.

8.Portability:
Many Traeger grill models are portable, making them perfect for camping, tailgating, or any outdoor activity.

9.Energy Efficiency:
Traeger grills use an efficient pellet delivery system that optimizes fuel consumption, making them cost-effective over time.

10.App Connectivity:
With the Traeger app, you can monitor and control the grill remotely, receive notifications, and access a library of recipes for endless cooking inspiration.

11.Safety:
The design and operation of Traeger grills are safer compared to traditional grills, reducing the risk of flare-ups and accidents.

12.Wide Variety of Pellet Flavors:
Traeger grills use hardwood pellets that come in a variety of flavors like Alder, Hickory, Oak, Apple, Maple, Cherry, Mesquite, and Pecan, allowing you to experiment with different taste profiles.

13.Community and Support:
Owning a Traeger grill gives you access to a large community of users and extensive customer support, providing tips, recipes, and assistance whenever needed.

By utilizing the Traeger Wood Fire Pellet Grill, you can enhance your cooking experience with these numerous benefits, making it a valuable addition to your culinary toolkit.

Step-by-Step Using It

1. Setup and Preheat
- Assemble the Grill: Follow the manufacturer's instructions to assemble your Traeger grill if it's new.
- Check the Hopper: Ensure the hopper is filled with the hardwood pellets of your choice.
- Plug in and Turn On: Connect your grill to a power source and turn it on using the main power switch.
- Set the Temperature: Use the digital controller to set your desired cooking temperature. The grill will begin to preheat, which typically takes 10-15 minutes.

2. Preparing the Grill
- Clean the Grill Grates: Make sure the grill grates are clean. Use a grill brush to remove any residue from previous cooking sessions.
- Season the Grates: Lightly oil the grates with cooking spray or a paper towel dipped in oil to prevent food from sticking.

3. Preparing the Food
- Marinate and Season: Prepare your food by marinating and seasoning as desired. Whether it's meat, vegetables, or other items, make sure they're ready for grilling.
- Preheat Accessories: If using accessories like a cast iron skillet or pizza stone, place them on the grill to preheat.

4. Cooking
- Place the Food on the Grill: Once the grill has reached the desired temperature, place your food on the grill grates.
- Use the Meat Probe: Insert the meat probe into the thickest part of the meat to monitor internal temperature without opening the lid.
- Maintain the Temperature: Keep the grill lid closed as much as possible to maintain a consistent temperature and smoke level.

5. Monitoring and Adjusting
- Monitor with the App: If available, use the Traeger app to monitor and adjust the grill and food temperatures remotely.
- Check the Pellets: Periodically check the hopper to ensure there are enough pellets for continuous cooking.
- Rotate Food: For even cooking, occasionally rotate or flip your food as needed.

6. Finishing Up
- Check for Doneness: Use the meat probe or a separate thermometer to ensure your food has reached the desired internal temperature.
- Remove the Food: Once cooked, carefully remove your food from the grill and let it rest if necessary, especially for meats.
- Turn Off the Grill: Turn off the grill using the controller and let it cool down.

7. Cleaning and Maintenance
- Clean the Grill Grates: Once the grill has cooled, clean the grates with a grill brush.
- Empty the Drip Tray: Dispose of any grease and drippings from the drip tray.
- Vacuum the Firepot: Regularly vacuum out the firepot to remove ash and maintain efficient pellet burning.
- Store the Grill: If not using the grill for an extended period, cover it with a grill cover and store it in a dry place.

By following these step-by-step instructions, you can ensure a successful and enjoyable grilling experience with your Traeger Wood Fire Pellet Grill.

Tips and Tricks to Using Your Traeger Wood Fire Pellet Grill

Your Traeger Grill is not limited to just smoking meats. In fact, this versatile kitchen appliance can be used to prepare a wide array of dishes. From grilling vegetables and baking pizzas to roasting poultry and even baking desserts, the possibilities are endless. Ensure you're taking full advantage of your Traeger Grill's capabilities to explore and create a variety of delicious meals.

1. Preheat Your Grill:
Always preheat your Traeger grill for at least 10-15 minutes before cooking. This ensures the grill reaches the desired temperature and helps achieve even cooking.

2. Keep the Hopper Full:
Ensure the hopper is always filled with pellets to maintain consistent heat and smoke throughout the cooking process. This prevents interruptions and maintains the desired flavor.

3. Use the Right Pellets:
Experiment with different wood pellet flavors to enhance your dishes. Common options include Alder, Hickory, Oak, Apple, Maple, Cherry, Mesquite, and Pecan. Each type imparts a unique flavor.

4. Clean the Grill Regularly:
Regularly clean the grill grates, drip tray, and firepot to maintain optimal performance and prevent flare-ups. Remove ash build-up and grease to ensure even heating and flavor consistency.

5. Utilize the Meat Probe:
Use the meat probe to monitor the internal temperature of your food without opening the lid. This ensures precise cooking and helps you achieve the desired doneness.

6. Keep the Lid Closed:
Avoid opening the lid frequently. Every time you open the lid, heat and smoke escape, which can lead to longer cooking times and uneven cooking.

7. Use a Drip Pan Liner:
Line the drip pan with aluminum foil or use a disposable drip pan liner to make clean-up easier. This also helps in managing grease and drippings.

8. Adjust Smoke Levels:
For a stronger smoke flavor, cook at lower temperatures. For a milder smoke flavor, increase the cooking temperature. Experiment to find your preferred smoke intensity.

9. Cook Indirectly:
Use indirect cooking methods for larger cuts of meat or slow-cooked recipes. Place a heat shield or use the grill's built-in deflectors to create indirect heat zones.

10. Use the App:
Download the Traeger app to monitor and control your grill remotely. The app allows you to adjust temperatures, set timers, and receive alerts, making the cooking process more convenient.

11. Let Meat Rest:
Allow your meat to rest after cooking. This helps retain juices and results in more tender and flavorful meat.

12. Experiment with Recipes:
Traeger grills are versatile. Experiment with smoking, grilling, baking, roasting, and braising. Try different recipes to fully utilize your grill's capabilities.

13. Season Your Grill:

Season your grill by running it at high temperatures with a light coat of oil on the grates before the first use and periodically after cleaning. This helps maintain a non-stick surface and enhances flavor.

14. Maintain Consistent Pellet Supply:

Keep extra pellets on hand to ensure you don't run out during long cooks. Different recipes may require more pellets, so plan accordingly.

By following these tips and tricks, you can maximize the performance of your Traeger Wood Fire Pellet Grill and enjoy delicious, perfectly cooked meals every time.

Cleaning & Maintaining of Traeger Wood Fire Grills

Proper cleaning and maintenance are very important to keep your Traeger Wood Fire Pellet Grill performing at its best. Follow these steps to ensure your grill stays in top condition.

After Each Use

1. Clean the Grill Grates:

Brush Off Residue: Use a grill brush to remove food residue and grease from the grates while they are still warm.

Wipe Down Grates: After brushing, use a damp cloth or paper towel to wipe down the grates.

2. Empty the Drip Tray:

Dispose of Grease: Remove the drip tray and dispose of any grease and drippings.

Wipe Clean: Wipe the drip tray with a paper towel or cloth.

3. Check the Hopper:

Remove Excess Pellets: If you're not using the grill for an extended period, remove excess pellets from the hopper to prevent moisture absorption.

Monthly Maintenance

1. Deep Clean the Grill:

Remove Grill Grates and Drip Tray: Take out the grill grates, drip tray, and heat baffle.

Vacuum the Firepot: Use a shop vacuum to remove ash and debris from the firepot and the bottom of the grill.

2. Clean the Interior:

Scrape and Wipe Down: Use a scraper to remove any built-up grease and food particles from the interior walls. Wipe down with a damp cloth.

3. Clean the Grates and Heat Baffle:

Soak and Scrub: Soak the grates and heat baffle in warm soapy water. Use a scrub brush to remove any stubborn residue.

Rinse and Dry: Rinse thoroughly and dry completely before reinstalling.

4. Check the Gasket:

Inspect for Damage: Look at the door gasket to ensure it is not damaged or worn out.

Clean the Gasket: Wipe the gasket with a damp cloth to remove grease and debris.

1. Inspect Electrical Components:

Verify that all electrical connections are secure and free from corrosion.

Test Ignition: Test the ignition system to make sure it is functioning properly.

2. Lubricate Moving Parts:

Lubricate the Auger: Apply a small amount of food-safe lubricant to the auger motor and any other moving parts.

Annual Maintenance

1. Full Inspection:

Check for Wear and Tear: Inspect the entire grill for signs of wear and tear, such as rust or damaged components.

Replace Parts: Replace any worn-out or damaged parts as necessary.

2. Deep Clean the Exterior:

Wipe Down: Clean the exterior of the grill with a mild detergent and water. Avoid using abrasive cleaners.

Polish Stainless Steel: If your grill has stainless steel parts, use a stainless steel cleaner to polish and protect them.

1. Store in a Dry Place:

Cover the Grill: Use a grill cover to protect your grill from the elements.

Indoor Storage: If possible, store your grill in a garage or shed to keep it dry and protected.

2. Winterization:

Remove Pellets: Empty the hopper and clean the grill thoroughly before storing it for the winter.

Disconnect Power: Unplug the grill and store the power cord in a dry place.

By following these cleaning and maintenance steps, you can ensure your Traeger Wood Fire Pellet Grill remains in excellent condition, providing you with delicious, perfectly cooked meals for years to come.

1. Why won't my grill ignite?

Verify Power at the Electrical Outlet: Ensure the outlet has power. If the power cord is connected to a GFCI (ground fault circuit interrupter), check and reset it if necessary.

Initiate start-up. If there is no ignition, proceed to the

next step.

Check the Control and Fuse: DANGER! Turn the switch OFF and disconnect the power cord.

Remove the control and inspect the fuse on the back. Replace the fuse if it is blown. Reinstall the control panel.

Inspect Draft Inducer Fan and Auger Drive Motor: Verify that both the draft inducer fan and the auger drive motor are operating.

If both are functioning, the hot rod may need to be replaced.

If either or both are not operating, contact Traeger's VIP-365 Customer Service for further troubleshooting or to place an order.

Check Pellet Hopper: Ensure there are pellets in the pellet hopper.

If this is the initial firing or the grill has run out of pellets, allow up to 7 minutes for the pellets to travel from the hopper to the firepot.

Initiate start-up. If there are still no pellets in the firepot, proceed to next answer. If the auger drive motor is operating (check the small fan blade on the back of the motor), the problem is in the digital control, which will need to be replaced. Contact your Traeger dealer or Traeger's VIP-365 Customer Service.

2. Why are no pellets being delivered into the firepot?

If the auger drive motor is not operating but the draft inducer fan is operating, the problem is in the auger system, which will need to be checked: With the switch OFF, locate the small fan blade on the back of the auger drive motor.

CAUTION! While watching the fan blade, turn the switch ON. If the fan blade does not turn, turn the switch OFF. This indicates a defective auger drive motor, and it will need to be replaced. Contact your Traeger dealer or Traeger's VIP-365 Customer Service to place an order.

If the fan blade turns a bit and then stops, continue watching and turn the switch OFF. If the fan blade unwinds slightly, this indicates a jam in the auger system, which will need to be cleared.

DANGER! Turn the switch OFF and disconnect the

power cord. Remove the pellets from the pellet hopper. Check for foreign objects and wet or decomposed pellets, both of which can cause a jam in the auger system. The auger will need to be removed to clear a jam in the auger system. See "How do I remove the auger if it jams?" section on the following page.

3. Why is the temperature of my grill fluctuating?

Temperature fluctuations are normal for Traeger grills. Any significant fluctuation could be caused by wind, improper use, air temperature, or lack of grill maintenance.

4. How do I remove the auger if it jams?

DANGER! Turn the switch OFF and disconnect the power cord.

CAUTION! If the grill is still hot, allow it to cool thoroughly.

- Access the Auger Drive Motor: Remove any covers necessary to access the auger drive motor.
- Disconnect the Auger Drive Motor: Remove the screw connecting the auger drive motor shaft to the auger shaft. Remove the screw retaining the auger bushing into the auger tube.
- Free the Auger: Using a small pipe wrench or locking pliers on the auger shaft, turn the auger counterclockwise. It may turn hard initially until it breaks free, then it will turn freely.
- Clean the Auger and Components: Remove the auger and clean out all pellets, ash, or foreign objects from the auger, auger tube, and firepot. Sand the outside surfaces of the auger with medium grit sandpaper. Check the inside of the auger tube and sand it if needed. Vacuum the sanding grit out of the auger tube and firepot when finished.
- Check and Reassemble: Ensure the auger rotates freely. Reattach the auger shaft to the auger drive motor shaft.

5. How do I protect my paint finish?

Use a protective cover on the grill to protect your paint finish. A Traeger grill cover is highly recommended. Covers are available from your Traeger dealer, or log onto our website, traegergrills.com.

Every 90 days, use a high-quality car wax on the outside surfaces of the grill. ONLY APPLY WAX TO A COLD GRILL.

6. Where can I get a new part for my grill?
Check with your Traeger dealer. They may have the part in stock or can order the part for you.
Contact Traeger's VIP-365 Customer Service to place an order.
In either case, please provide your name, address, phone number, model, and serial number of the grill (located on the label inside the hopper lid), along with the part identification number from the component diagram or parts list.

Conclusion

In wrapping up this comprehensive guide to the Traeger Wood Fire Pellet Grill, it's clear that this versatile and powerful appliance is a game-changer for both novice and experienced grill enthusiasts. Throughout this cookbook, we've explored a myriad of recipes that showcase the grill's ability to grill, smoke, roast, bake, braise, and BBQ with ease, all while infusing your dishes with that signature wood-fired flavor.

The Traeger grill's ability to maintain consistent temperatures, its ease of use, and the enhanced flavors it imparts to food make it a standout choice for any cooking enthusiast. Whether you're preparing a weeknight dinner or hosting a large backyard barbecue, the Traeger grill proves to be an invaluable tool. Its user-friendly design, coupled with the ability to control and monitor cooking through the Traeger app, makes the cooking process not only efficient but also enjoyable.

We've also covered the essential tips and tricks to maximize your grilling experience, from selecting the right type of wood pellets to maintaining your grill in top condition. Proper care and maintenance ensure that your grill continues to perform at its best, providing you with delicious meals and reliable service for years to come.

This cookbook has been designed to provide you with not only recipes but also the knowledge and confidence to experiment and create your own culinary masterpieces. The versatility of the Traeger Wood Fire Pellet Grill enables you to explore a wide range of cooking techniques and flavors, making it an essential part of your kitchen arsenal.

As you continue your grilling journey, remember that the key to great cooking lies in enjoying the process and experimenting with different flavors and techniques. The Traeger Wood Fire Pellet Grill is designed to make this journey as enjoyable and rewarding as possible. Happy grilling, and may your culinary adventures be filled with delicious discoveries and unforgettable meals.

4-Week Meal Plan

Week 1

Day 1:
Breakfast: Cream Cheese Zucchini Baguette Sandwiches
Lunch: Crispy Potato Wedges
Dinner: Lemon-Honey Glazed Chicken Breasts

Day 2:
Breakfast: Garlic Bread with Sun-Dried Tomatoes
Lunch: Spicy Black Turtle Beans
Dinner: Garlicky Prime Rib Roast

Day 3:
Breakfast: Potato and Peas Frittata
Lunch: Eggplant Cucumber Salad
Dinner: Grilled Cajun Mahi-Mahi

Day 4:
Breakfast: Cheesy Biscuit and Gravy Breakfast Bake
Lunch: Lemon Broccoli with Parmesan
Dinner: Smoked Chicken Gumbo with Rice

Day 5:
Breakfast: Beer and Cheese Bread
Lunch: Balsamic Brussels Sprouts with Pomegranate Seeds, Walnuts, and Grapes
Dinner: Grilled Flank Steak with Chimichurri

Day 6:
Breakfast: Strawberry Pancake
Lunch: Garlic Bok Choy with Sesame Seeds
Dinner: Cedar-Plank Grilled Salmon

Day 7:
Breakfast: Biscuit Breakfast Sausage Pudding
Lunch: Asian-Spiced Bok Choy
Dinner: Barbecue Pork Riblets

Week 2

Day 1:
Breakfast: Pancetta Onion Frittata
Lunch: Southern Baked Beans
Dinner: Herb-Smoked Whole Turkey

Day 2:
Breakfast: Delicious Naan
Lunch: Grilled Corn on the Cob
Dinner: Roast Beef, Potato and Egg Skillet

Day 3:
Breakfast: Deviled Eggs
Lunch: Grilled Italian-Style Portabellas
Dinner: Grilled Oysters with Lemon-Garlic Sauce

Day 4:
Breakfast: Homemade Pita Bread
Lunch: Asian-Inspired Coleslaw
Dinner: Spicy Lemongrass Chicken with Cilantro Pesto

Day 5:
Breakfast: No-Knead Bread
Lunch: Pico De Gallo
Dinner: Sweet and Sour Short Ribs

Day 6:
Breakfast: Classic Shakshouka
Lunch: Grilled Beets with Goat Cheese, Arugula, and Pistachios
Dinner: Savory Crab Cakes with Spicy Mayo

Day 7:
Breakfast: Cornbread
Lunch: Balsamic Portabello Mushroom & Cheese Panini
Dinner: Greek Pork Souvlaki

Week 3

Day 1:
Breakfast: Sweet Country Sausage Baked Beans
Lunch: Garlic Leek and White Beans Casserole
Dinner: Spicy Chicken Drumsticks

Day 2:
Breakfast: Bacon and Butternut Squash Bread Pudding
Lunch: Grilled Eggplant with Sun-Dried Tomato Vinaigrette
Dinner: Grilled Hot Dogs with Spicy Pickled Vegetables

Day 3:
Breakfast: Cheese Asparagus and Tomato Frittata
Lunch: Apple-Cabbage Slaw
Dinner: Lemon Garlic Lobster Tail Skewers

Day 4:
Breakfast: Fluffy Corn Bread
Lunch: Charred Asparagus with Basil-Lime Sauce
Dinner: Garlic-Sage Turkey Cutlets with Cranberry-Apple Sauce

Day 5:
Breakfast: Garlic Bread with Sun-Dried Tomatoes
Lunch: Simple Smoked Spaghetti Squash
Dinner: Flavorful Pepper Steak Stir-Fry

Day 6:
Breakfast: Cream Cheese Zucchini Baguette Sandwiches
Lunch: Savory Cauliflower Steaks
Dinner: Hearty Shrimp, Chicken, and Sausage Paella

Day 7:
Breakfast: Cheesy Biscuit and Gravy Breakfast Bake
Lunch: Teriyaki Onion Pops
Dinner: Rosemary-Garlic Rack of Lamb

Week 4

Day 1:
Breakfast: Beer and Cheese Bread
Lunch: Beer Slow-Cooked Pinto Beans
Dinner: Teriyaki Chicken Skewers

Day 2:
Breakfast: Strawberry Pancake
Lunch: Savory Jerk-Marinated Tofu
Dinner: Grilled T-Bone Steaks with Moroccan Spice Paste

Day 3:
Breakfast: Biscuit Breakfast Sausage Pudding
Lunch: Cheese Corn and Pepper Salad
Dinner: Tuna Sliders with Wasabi Broccoli Slaw

Day 4:
Breakfast: Pancetta Onion Frittata
Lunch: Crispy Sweet Potato Wedges
Dinner: Salty and Sweet Turkey Legs

Day 5:
Breakfast: Delicious Naan
Lunch: Grilled Pancetta-Wrapped Asparagus
Dinner: Grilled Meat Loaf

Day 6:
Breakfast: Homemade Pita Bread
Lunch: Balsamic Turnip Wedges with Goat Cheese
Dinner: Blackened Tilapia Tacos

Day 7:
Breakfast: Classic Shakshouka
Lunch: Grilled Zucchini with Basil and Orange Zest
Dinner: Venison Steaks with Blackberry Sauce

Chapter 1 Breakfast Recipes

14   Garlic Bread with Sun-Dried Tomatoes

14   Cream Cheese Zucchini Baguette
      Sandwiches

14   Deviled Eggs

15   Potato and Peas Frittata

15   Strawberry Pancake

15   Sweet Country Sausage Baked Beans

16   Biscuit Breakfast Sausage Pudding

16   Pancetta Onion Frittata

16   Cheesy Biscuit and Gravy Breakfast
      Bake

17   Homemade Pita Bread

17   No-Knead Bread

17   Cornbread

18   Fluffy Corn Bread

18   Bacon and Butternut Squash Bread
      Pudding

18   Classic Shakshouka

19   Delicious Naan

19   Beer and Cheese Bread

20   Cheese Asparagus and Tomato Frittata

Garlic Bread with Sun-Dried Tomatoes

Prep Time: 10 minutes | Cook Time: 10 minutes | Serves: 10

½ cup sun-dried tomatoes packed in oil
8 garlic cloves, minced or pushed through a press
1 teaspoon dried oregano
¼ teaspoon crushed red pepper flakes

2 tablespoons unsalted butter, softened
1 loaf French or Italian bread, about 1 pound, cut crosswise in half, each half cut lengthwise to make 4 pieces
1½ cups grated Mexican-style cheese blend (6 ounces)

1. When ready to cook, set Traeger temperature to 400°F and preheat, lid closed for 15 minutes. 2. Drain the tomatoes, reserve 3 tablespoons of the oil, and chop the tomatoes. In a small skillet over medium heat, warm the reserved oil. Add the garlic, oregano, and red pepper flakes, and cook until the garlic just barely starts to brown, 2½ to 3 minutes, stirring occasionally. Remove from the heat and transfer to a medium bowl. Add the butter and stir until the butter is melted and the mixture is well combined. 3. Tear off two long sheets of aluminum foil and place two bread pieces, cut side up, on each piece. Brush with an equal amount of the butter mixture, and then close the bread like a sandwich, with the cut sides facing each other. Wrap the bread in the foil and place in the grill grate. 4. Close the lid and cook for 5 to 8 minutes, turning every 2 minutes. Remove from the grill, open the foil, and set the bread halves, cut side up, next to each other on the foil. Top with the cheese and the sun-dried tomatoes. 5. Return the bread to the grill grate, leaving the halves on top of the foil and unwrapped. Grill at 350°F until the cheese melts, 4 to 6 minutes. Remove from the grill and cut into 2-inch pieces. Serve warm or at room temperature.

Cream Cheese Zucchini Baguette Sandwiches

Prep Time: 15 minutes | Cook Time: 4 minutes | Serves: 4

3 tablespoons extra-virgin olive oil
½ teaspoon dried oregano
½ teaspoon kosher salt
¼ teaspoon freshly ground black pepper
1½ pounds green and/or yellow zucchini, ends trimmed, cut lengthwise into ¼-inch slices
½ cup whipped cream cheese, softened
⅓ cup store-bought basil pesto

Finely grated zest of 1 lemon
5 fresh basil leaves, finely chopped (optional)
1 French baguette, about 8 ounces, cut crosswise into 4 pieces, each halved horizontally
8 ounces roasted red bell peppers (in a jar), drained and cut into flat strips
4 ounces smoked Gouda, provolone, or mozzarella cheese, cut into thin slices

1. In a baking dish, whisk the oil, oregano, salt, and pepper. Add the zucchini and turn to coat evenly. Set aside at room temperature. 2. Combine the cream cheese, pesto, lemon zest, and basil (if using). 3. When ready to cook, set Traeger temperature to 400°F and preheat, lid closed for 15 minutes. 4. Place the baking dish directly on the grill grate. Close the lid and cook for 4 minutes, turning once or twice. During the last minute of grilling time, toast the baguette pieces, cut side down, on the grill grate. Remove the zucchini and the baguette pieces from the grill. 5. Spread a thin layer of the cream cheese mixture over the cut side of each baguette piece. Build the sandwiches with equal amounts of the zucchini, bell peppers, and cheese. Serve warm.

Deviled Eggs

Prep Time: 20 minutes | Cook Time: 45 minutes | Serves: 12

12 eggs
½ cup mayonnaise
½ cup yellow mustard

Kosher salt
Freshly ground black pepper
1 teaspoon paprika

1. Gently place the eggs in a large pot and cover with water. Bring to a boil, then reduce the heat to low and simmer for 10 minutes. Turn the stove off and let the eggs sit in the hot water for 45 minutes. 2. When ready to cook, set Traeger temperature to 180°F and preheat, lid closed for 15 minutes. 3. Place a few ice cubes in the water with the eggs to cool them slightly, but they should still be warm and easy to peel. Peel the eggs and place them on the grill grate for 45 minutes. 4. Cut the eggs in half lengthwise, remove the yolks, and put the yolks in a large bowl. Place the whites, cut-side up, on a tray. 5. In the bowl with the yolks, add the mayonnaise, mustard, and a pinch each of salt and pepper. Beat with a hand mixer for 1 minute, and taste to adjust seasoning. Divide this mixture evenly among each egg white. 6. Sprinkle with the paprika and store in the refrigerator until ready to serve.

Potato and Peas Frittata

Prep Time: 30 minutes | Cook Time: 25 minutes | Serves: 4

8 large eggs
Kosher salt
Freshly ground black pepper
2 tablespoons extra-virgin olive oil
8 ounces baby Yukon gold potatoes, unpeeled, scrubbed, and thinly sliced (about 2 cups)
½ large red onion, thinly sliced (about 1 ¼ cups)

1 medium red bell pepper, cut into thin strips
2 teaspoons smoked paprika, divided
1 cup frozen petite peas, thawed
2 medium garlic cloves, minced or pushed through a press
2 ½ ounces soft garlic-and-herb cheese, broken into small pieces
2 tablespoons finely chopped fresh Italian parsley leaves
2 tablespoons capers, rinsed and drained

1. Set Traeger temperature to 400°F and preheat, lid closed for 15 minutes. 2. Whisk the eggs with ½ teaspoon salt and ¼ teaspoon pepper. 3. Add the oil to a 9-inch cast-iron skillet and then add the potatoes, onion, and bell pepper. Place the skillet directly on the grill grate. Close the lid and cook for 1 minute, stirring occasionally. Season evenly with 1 teaspoon salt, ½ teaspoon pepper, and 1½ teaspoons of the paprika and stir to combine. Continue cooking, with the lid closed, until the potatoes are tender when pierced with a fork and the vegetables are lightly browned, 13 to 15 minutes, stirring frequently so that the vegetables cook evenly and don't stick to the skillet. Add the peas and the garlic and cook for 1 to 2 minutes more. 4. Spread the vegetables evenly in the skillet. Pour the eggs on top of the vegetables and then add the cheese. Cook with the lid closed, until the eggs are puffed and just firm in the center, 10 to 13 minutes, lowering the temperature if needed to prevent the frittata from getting too brown on the bottom. 5. Wearing insulated barbecue mitts, remove the skillet from the grill. Top evenly with the parsley, the remaining ½ teaspoon paprika, and the capers. Serve the frittata from the skillet, either warm or at room temperature.

Strawberry Pancake

Prep Time: 10 minutes | Cook Time: 25 minutes | Serves: 4

3 tablespoons confectioners' sugar, plus more for serving
1 cup chopped ripe strawberries
3 tablespoons unsalted butter, divided
3 tablespoons firmly packed light brown sugar
8 large eggs
1 (3-ounce) package cream cheese, softened

1 cup whole milk
3 tablespoons honey
1 cup all-purpose flour
½ teaspoon kosher salt
½ teaspoon baking powder
¼ teaspoon ground cinnamon

1. In a medium bowl, combine the confectioners' sugar and strawberries and toss to coat. Set aside. 2. Set Traeger temperature to 425°F and preheat, lid closed for 15 minutes. 3. Take 1 tablespoon of the butter and smear it over the bottom and sides of a 12-inch cast-iron skillet. Dust the butter with the brown sugar, shaking out any excess. Place the remaining 2 tablespoons butter in the skillet and set aside. 4. Place the eggs, cream cheese, milk, honey, flour, salt, baking powder, and cinnamon in a blender or food processor and puree until smooth and batter-like. 5. Place the skillet on the grill grate, close the lid, and let the skillet preheat for about 5 minutes. Open the lid and pour in the batter. Close the lid and bake until puffed up and golden brown, 20 to 25 minutes. 6. Remove the skillet from the grill and dust the pancake with confectioners' sugar. Cut into servings and spoon the strawberries over each serving.

Sweet Country Sausage Baked Beans

Prep Time: 10 minutes | Cook Time: 1 hour | Serves: 8

3 (32-ounce) cans pork and beans, drained
2 pounds country breakfast sausage, browned and crumbled
2 medium onions, thinly sliced into half moons
1 cup firmly packed light brown sugar

1 cup dark corn syrup
¼ cup prepared yellow mustard
1 tablespoon dry mustard
2 teaspoons Worcestershire sauce

1. When ready to cook, set Traeger temperature to 350°F and preheat, lid closed for 15 minutes. 2. Pour the drained pork and beans in a 9- × 13-inch disposable aluminum-foil baking pan. Add the sausage and onions and stir to mix. Add the remaining ingredients and stir to blend well. 3. Set the baking pan on the grill grate, close the lid, and bake for at least 1 hour; 1½ hours is better. Cooking the beans the day before and reheating them for about 30 minutes in a preheated 350° F oven will get you the very best flavor.

Biscuit Breakfast Sausage Pudding

Prep Time: 10 minutes | Cook Time: 35 minutes | Serves: 8

20 to 24 baked tea biscuits or 8 baked regular biscuits (baked frozen biscuits are okay)
1-pound mild or hot country breakfast sausage
3 tablespoons all-purpose flour
2 cups whole milk

Freshly ground black pepper
6 large eggs, beaten
1 cup shredded cheese (I like a mixture of cheddar and Gruyère)
Maple syrup for serving

1. Line the bottom of a 15-inch cast-iron baking pan with the biscuits. You should have some left to crumble on top. 2. In a large skillet over medium heat, brown the sausage, using a spatula to break apart large chunks. This will take 8 to 10 minutes. Once all the pink is gone, sprinkle in the flour and stir to coat the sausage. Continue to cook for another 1 to 2 minutes. Slowly start stirring in the milk. You may not need the entire 2 cups. You want the gravy to build and thicken but not be too thick; this usually takes about 5 minutes. Season to taste with pepper. Spoon the gravy evenly over the biscuits. Use all the gravy. Pour the beaten eggs over the top. Crumble the remaining biscuits over the eggs. Scatter the cheese evenly over everything. 3. When ready to cook, set Traeger temperature to 350°F and preheat, lid closed for 15 minutes. 4. Place the baking pan on the grill grate, close the lid, and bake until the cheese has browned a bit and the center of the pudding feels a little firm to the touch, but is still slightly liquid, 20 to 25 minutes. 5. Remove the pan from the grill and let sit 10 minutes. Cut into serving pieces and drizzle with maple syrup if desired. Serve immediately.

Pancetta Onion Frittata

Prep Time: 10 minutes | Cook Time: 35 minutes | Serves: 6

8 large eggs
2 tablespoons milk
1 cup shredded fontina cheese
Kosher salt and freshly ground black pepper

1 tablespoon unsalted butter
½ cup diced onion
4 ounces pancetta, diced
¼ cup sour cream for serving (optional)

1. When ready to cook, set Traeger temperature to 400°F and preheat, lid closed for 15 minutes. 2. In a large bowl, whisk the eggs, milk, cheese, and salt and pepper to taste together. 3. In a 12-inch cast-iron skillet over medium heat, melt the butter; when it foams, add the onion and cook until it is soft and some color develops, about 10 minutes, stirring occasionally. Add the pancetta and cook, stirring a few times, until it takes on a little color, about 5 minutes. Pour the egg mixture into the pan and stir it around with a spatula so that the eggs make full contact with the bottom of the pan. 4. Immediately, take the pan and place it on the grill grate. Close the lid and bake until the frittata is puffed up and golden brown, 20 to 25 minutes. 5. Remove the skillet from the grill and let cool for about 10 minutes. Slice the frittata into wedges and serve with sour cream, if desired.

Cheesy Biscuit and Gravy Breakfast Bake

Prep Time: 40 minutes | Cook Time: 50 minutes | Serves: 10

8 tablespoons (1 stick) unsalted butter
½ cup all-purpose flour
6½ cups milk, divided
1 onion, chopped
2 tablespoons minced garlic
1 tablespoon Worcestershire sauce
2 teaspoons hot sauce
2 teaspoons red pepper flakes

2 teaspoons salt
2 teaspoons freshly ground black pepper
2 pounds ground sausage, cooked and crumbled
1 (20-ounce) package shredded hash brown potatoes
20 refrigerated or thawed frozen biscuits
2 cups shredded sharp Cheddar cheese
10 eggs, beaten
Nonstick cooking spray or butter, for greasing

1. On the stove top, in a skillet over medium heat, melt the butter. 2. Whisk in the flour, stirring constantly for 1 minute. 3. Gradually add 6 cups of milk, the onion, garlic, Worcestershire sauce, hot sauce, red pepper flakes, salt, and pepper. 4. Continue cooking for 2 minutes, then fold in the cooked sausage; set the mixture aside. 5. When ready to cook, set Traeger temperature to 350°F and preheat, lid closed for 15 minutes. 6. Line a 9-by-13-inch baking pan with aluminum foil and coat with cooking spray. 7. Spread the hash browns in the bottom of the pan and top with the biscuits. Cover with the shredded cheese. 8. In a medium bowl, combine the beaten eggs and remaining ½ cup of milk. Pour this mixture over the cheese in the pan, then top with the sausage gravy. 9. Place the pan on the grill grate, close the lid, and grill for 45 minutes, or until bubbly.

Homemade Pita Bread

Prep Time: 15 minutes | Cook Time: 6 minutes | Serves: 8

1½ cups unbleached all-purpose flour
½ cup whole wheat flour
2 teaspoons regular table salt, not kosher

2 teaspoons instant yeast
2 tablespoons olive oil
1¼ cups warm water (105° to 110° F)

1. Make the dough at least 1½ hours before baking. This will yield better flavor. In the bowl of a stand mixer fitted with a paddle attachment, combine all of the ingredients and mix on low speed until the flour is fully moistened. This will take less than a minute. Change to the dough hook and let the machine run on medium speed for about 10 minutes. The dough will clean the bowl and be smooth, soft, and a little sticky. 2. Spray the inside of a large bowl with cooking spray. Place the dough in the bowl and lightly spray the top. Cover with plastic wrap and let rise at room temperature until the dough doubles in size. This will take about 1½ hours, but you can let the dough continue to rise for up to 8 hours. You can refrigerate the risen dough for up to 3 days. 3. Transfer the dough to a lightly floured work surface and cut it into 8 to 12 equal pieces. Work with one piece at a time, keeping the rest covered with a damp cloth. Shape each piece into a ball and then flatten it into a disc. Cover the dough with plastic wrap sprayed with cooking spray and let rest for 20 minutes at room temperature. 4. When ready to cook, set Traeger temperature to 475°F and preheat, lid closed for 15 minutes. 5. Roll each disc into a circle about ¼ inch thick. Allow them to rest for 10 minutes, uncovered, before grilling. 6. Quickly place as many pieces of dough on the grill grate, about an inch apart. If they don't drop into perfect circles, don't worry, they will still taste good. Close the lid and cook for about 3 minutes. Turn the pitas, close the lid, and cook for another 2 to 3 minutes. They may puff up; if they do, flatten them with a spatula. They're ready to come off the grill when they just turn from a raw flour look to a light brown with probably a few darker spots in places. 7. Transfer the grilled pitas to a clean kitchen towel and wrap them up. Continue until all the pitas are cooked. Serve hot or, when completely cool, store in a zip-top plastic bag for up to 3 days or in the freezer for up to 2 months. The pitas can be reheated for about 30 seconds in a hot oven before serving.

No-Knead Bread

Prep Time: 10 minutes | Cook Time: 45 minutes | Serves: 2

3 cups unbleached all-purpose flour
2 teaspoons regular table salt, not kosher

1 teaspoon active dry yeast
1⅔ cups warm water (105° to 110° F)

1. In a large bowl, combine the flour, salt, and yeast and mix well. Stir in the water until you have a very sticky, shaggy-looking dough. Cover with plastic wrap and let rise in the refrigerator for 18 to 24 hours. 2. Flour the work surface. Remove the plastic wrap from the bowl. The dough will have risen and be covered with bubbles. Transfer the dough to the work surface and dust the top with flour. Fold the dough in half, form it into a ball by stretching and tucking the edges of the dough underneath it. Flour a kitchen towel and place the dough on it. Top with another floured towel; let rise until doubled in size, about 2 hours. 3. When ready to cook, set Traeger temperature to 450°F and preheat, lid closed for 15 minutes. 4. Gently turn the dough ball onto the baking stone, seam side down. Cover the dough with a large metal mixing bowl. Close the lid and bake for 30 minutes. Remove the bowl and continue to bake until the crust is golden brown, 15 to 20 minutes. You can also judge doneness by taking the internal temperature of the bread, which should be 110° F. 5. Transfer the bread to a wire rack and let cool before slicing—if you can wait that long.

Cornbread

Prep Time: 10 minutes | Cook Time: 25 minutes | Serves: 8

2 cups self-rising cornmeal mix
1⅓ cups buttermilk
1 to 2 tablespoons sugar (optional)

¼ cup corn oil
1 large egg, slightly beaten

1. Spray an 8-inch cast-iron skillet with 2-inch sides with cooking spray. 2. Set Traeger temperature to 375°F and preheat, lid closed for 15 minutes. 3. In a large bowl, whisk the cornmeal mix, buttermilk, oil, egg, and sugar, if using, together. 4. Place the prepared skillet on the grill grate and close the lid. Pour the batter into the heated skillet. Close the lid and bake until the cornbread pulls away from the side of the skillet and a toothpick inserted in the center comes out clean, 25 to 30 minutes. 5. Remove the skillet from the grill, cut the cornbread into 8 wedges or squares, and serve hot.

Fluffy Corn Bread

Prep Time: 15 minutes | Cook Time: 1 hour | Serves: 8

½ cup corn oil, plus ½ tablespoon
1 cup yellow cornmeal
1¼ cups all-purpose flour
½ cup granulated sugar
1 tablespoon baking powder
1 teaspoon baking soda

½ teaspoon flaked sea salt
1 cup buttermilk
¼ cup clover honey
3 tablespoons unsalted butter, melted
2 large eggs, lightly beaten
1 cup corn kernels

1. When ready to cook, set Traeger temperature to 275°F and preheat, lid closed for 15 minutes. 2. Brush a large cast iron skillet with ½ tablespoon of the corn oil. Set aside. 3. In a medium bowl, whisk together the cornmeal, flour, sugar, baking powder, baking soda, and salt. 4. In a large bowl, whisk together the buttermilk, remaining ½ cup of corn oil, honey, melted butter, and eggs until smooth. 5. Pour the dry ingredients into the wet ingredients and fold to combine. Do not overmix the batter. Pour the batter into the prepared skillet and smooth the top. Scatter the corn kernels over the top. Place the skillet on the grill grate smoke for 1 hour, or until a toothpick inserted into the thickest part of the corn bread comes out clean.

Bacon and Butternut Squash Bread Pudding

Prep Time: 30 minutes | Cook Time: 2 hours | Serves: 8

1-pound bacon slices, cut into ½-inch pieces
6 large eggs, lightly beaten
2 cups heavy (whipping) cream
3 thyme sprigs, leaves stripped and finely chopped
Flaked sea salt
Freshly ground black pepper

1 large butternut squash, peeled, halved lengthwise, seeded, and diced
3 leeks, white parts only, quartered lengthwise and thinly sliced
1 baguette loaf, diced
2 cups finely grated Parmesan cheese

1. When ready to cook, set Traeger temperature to 275°F and preheat, lid closed for 15 minutes. 2. Place a large cast iron casserole on the grill grate to preheat. Cook the bacon in the casserole for 30 minutes, or until golden brown, tossing occasionally. Spoon off and discard the excess fat. 3. In a large bowl, whisk together the eggs, heavy cream, and thyme leaves. Season with salt and pepper. Set aside. 4. Add the butternut squash and leeks to the casserole. Season with salt and pepper. Cook for 30 minutes. 5. Add the bread cubes to the casserole and gently fold them into the squash and leeks. 6. Pour the egg mixture evenly over the casserole ingredients. Top with the Parmesan cheese and season with salt and pepper (keep in mind the Parmesan is quite salty). Cook for 1 hour, or until golden brown and fully set. Let cool slightly before serving.

Classic Shakshouka

Prep Time: 15 minutes | Cook Time: 40 minutes | Serves: 4

1 tablespoon extra-virgin olive oil
1 medium onion, chopped
3 garlic cloves, chopped
2 medium bell peppers, seeded and chopped
1 large tomato, chopped
2 teaspoons cumin seeds
1 teaspoon ground coriander

½ teaspoon cayenne pepper
Kosher salt
Freshly ground black pepper
1 (15-ounce) can diced tomatoes
4 large eggs
½ cup crumbled feta cheese (optional)
¼ cup chopped fresh mint or flat-leaf parsley

1. When ready to cook, set Traeger temperature to 4000°F and preheat a 10-inch cast iron skillet on the grate with the grill lid closed. 2. Pour the oil into the skillet and close the grill lid. Once hot, add the onion, garlic, peppers, chopped tomato, cumin seeds, coriander, and cayenne. Season with salt and pepper and stir to combine. Close the lid and cook, stirring once or twice, for 24 to 28 minutes or until softened. 3. Stir in the diced tomatoes with their juice. Close the lid and cook for 9 to 12 minutes or until thickened slightly. 4. Form four wells in the sauce and add one egg to each well. Close the lid and cook for 4 to 6 minutes or until the whites have set but the yolks are still runny. 5. Remove from the heat, sprinkle with the feta (if using) and mint, and serve immediately.

Delicious Naan

Prep Time: 15 minutes | Cook Time: 6 minutes | Serves: 10

1 (¼-ounce) package active dry yeast
1 cup warm water (105° to 110° F)
¼ cup sugar
3 tablespoons whole milk
1 large egg, beaten
2 teaspoons regular table salt, not kosher

2 cups whole wheat flour
2½ cups bread flour
¼ cup (½ stick) unsalted butter, melted
Kosher salt
Middle Eastern Za'tar Seasoning, optional

1. In the bowl of a stand mixer fitted with a dough hook, dissolve the yeast in the warm water and let stand until frothy, about 10 minutes. On low speed, mix in the sugar, milk, egg, regular salt, and whole wheat flour. As that mixes, slowly add in the bread flour. Turn the mixer speed up one notch and let the machine knead the dough for 6 to 8 minutes, until you have a smooth dough that attaches itself to the dough hook. 2. Transfer the dough to a greased bowl. Cover with a damp cloth and let rise until doubled in volume, about 1 hour. 3. Punch down the dough and pinch off golf ball–size portions. Roll these into balls and place on a baking sheet. Cover with a clean kitchen towel and let rise until doubled in size, about 30 minutes. 4. When ready to cook, set Traeger temperature to 500°F and preheat, lid closed for 15 minutes. 5. On a floured work surface with a floured rolling pin, roll each ball of dough into a circle about ¼ inch thick. Place as many pieces of dough on the grill grate, close the lid, and cook for 2 to 3 minutes. Turn the pieces, close the lid, and cook for another 2 to 4 minutes, until nicely browned. 6. As you remove the naan from the grill, brush with the butter and sprinkle with kosher salt and za'tar if using. Continue until all the naan has been baked. You can freeze the dough for later use if desired. Just let the balls thaw and rise before cooking. Naan is best eaten hot but you can store leftovers in a zip-top bag for a couple of days; just reheat in your oven before serving.

Beer and Cheese Bread

Prep Time: 20 minutes | Cook Time: 1¼ hour | Serves: 8

1 bottle (12 ounces) dark beer, at room temperature
2 tablespoons granulated sugar
2 tablespoons unsalted butter, softened, plus more for the bowl
1 package (¼ ounce) instant, quick-rising yeast
1½ teaspoons table salt
1½ teaspoons dried thyme

½ teaspoon granulated garlic
½ teaspoon granulated onion
¼ teaspoon crushed red pepper flakes
4 ½ cups unbleached, all-purpose flour, plus more as needed
4 ounces sharp cheddar cheese, diced
Extra-virgin olive oil

1. In the bowl of a stand mixer, mix the beer, sugar, 2 tablespoons butter, yeast, salt, thyme, granulated garlic, granulated onion, and red pepper flakes. Attach the bowl to the mixer and affix the paddle beater. With the mixer on low speed, gradually add enough flour to form a soft dough that doesn't stick to the bowl. Turn off the mixer, cover the bowl with a towel, and let it rest for 10 minutes. Then, switch from the paddle attachment to the dough hook. With the mixer on medium-low speed, knead the dough, adding more flour as needed to keep it from sticking, until the dough is smooth and elastic, about 8 minutes. 2. Grease a large bowl with butter. Shape the dough into a ball. Put the dough in the bowl, smooth side down, and then turn smooth side up, coating the dough with butter. Cover with plastic wrap and let stand in a warm, draft-free place until the dough is doubled in volume, about 1½ hours. 3. Place a 12-inch square of parchment paper on a pizza peel (or a rimless baking sheet). Set aside. 4. On a lightly floured surface, gently roll the dough into a 13-by-9-inch rectangle. Scatter the cheese over the dough. Starting at a short end, roll the dough to enclose the cheese. Tuck the ends of the dough underneath the mass, and shape the dough into a ball. Place the dough, smooth side up, on the parchment-lined pizza peel. Coat a large piece of plastic wrap with oil. Cover the dough loosely with the plastic wrap, oiled side down, and let stand in a warm, draft-free place until the loaf looks inflated, but not doubled, about 45 minutes. Remove the plastic wrap. 5. When ready to cook, set Traeger temperature to 375°F and preheat a pizza stone, lid closed for 15 minutes. 6. Fill a spray bottle with water. Slide the loaf with the parchment paper onto the pizza stone. Quickly spray the surface of the loaf with water. Grill until the bread is golden brown and sounds hollow when tapped on the bottom, 1¼ to 1½ hours. (Some cheese may ooze onto the stone.) Remove the loaf from the stone, transfer to a wire cooling rack, and let cool for at least 30 minutes before cutting into slices.

Cheese Asparagus and Tomato Frittata

Prep Time: 20 minutes | Cook Time: 17 minutes | Serves: 6

8 ounces asparagus
6 large eggs
¼ cup half-and-half
¼ cup freshly grated Parmigiano-Reggiano® cheese (scant 1 ounce)
¼ teaspoon kosher salt

¼ teaspoon freshly ground black pepper
1 tablespoon extra-virgin olive oil
2 garlic cloves, finely chopped
1 cup ripe cherry tomatoes, cut in half crosswise
6 ounces feta cheese, crumbled (scant 1¼ cups)

1. One at a time grasp the end of each asparagus spear and bend it gently until it snaps at its natural point of tenderness, usually about two-thirds of the way down the spear. Discard the tough ends. Cut the spears on the diagonal into 1-inch pieces. Set aside. 2. In a blender, combine the eggs, half-and-half, Parmigiano-Reggiano®, salt, and pepper and process for 10 seconds to blend thoroughly. Set aside. 3. When ready to cook, set Traeger temperature to 400°F and preheat, lid closed for 15 minutes. 4. Preheat a 10-inch grill-proof skillet, preferably nonstick, on the grill grate, with the lid closed, for 3 minutes. Add the oil to the skillet and then add the asparagus and stir briefly to coat with the oil. Cook with the lid closed, for 2 minutes. Remove the skillet from the grill and roll the asparagus around in the skillet so the oil coats the bottom and sides of the pan evenly. Place the skillet back on the grill grate, arrange the asparagus in an even layer, and then scatter the garlic, tomatoes, and feta evenly over the asparagus. Pour the egg mixture into the skillet. Grill the frittata for 15 minutes with the lid closed, until the eggs are puffed, browned, and firm in the center. Remove from the grill. 5. Slide the frittata out of the skillet onto a serving plate. Cut into wedges and serve immediately.

Chapter 2 Vegetables and Sides Recipes

22 Crispy Potato Wedges

22 Southern Baked Beans

22 Balsamic Brussels Sprouts with Pomegranate Seeds, Walnuts, and Grapes

23 Garlic Leek and White Beans Casserole

23 Eggplant Cucumber Salad

23 Spicy Black Turtle Beans

24 Lemon Broccoli with Parmesan

24 Balsamic Portabello Mushroom & Cheese Panini

24 Asian-Spiced Bok Choy

25 Grilled Corn on the Cob

25 Grilled Italian-Style Portabellas

25 Asian-Inspired Coleslaw

26 Pico De Gallo

26 Beer Slow-Cooked Pinto Beans

26 Grilled Beets with Goat Cheese, Arugula, and Pistachios

27 Grilled Eggplant with Sun-Dried Tomato Vinaigrette

27 Garlic Bok Choy with Sesame Seeds

27 Apple-Cabbage Slaw

28 Charred Asparagus with Basil-Lime Sauce

28 Tuscan-Style Cannellini Beans

28 Teriyaki Onion Pops

29 Savory Jerk-Marinated Tofu

29 Savory Cauliflower Steaks

29 Cheese Corn and Pepper Salad

30 Simple Smoked Spaghetti Squash

30 Crispy Sweet Potato Wedges

30 Grilled Romaine Hearts Caesar Salad

31 Eggplant Slices with Spicy Dressing

31 Grilled Butter Carrots

31 Cheese Potatoes

32 Grilled Pancetta-Wrapped Asparagus

32 Balsamic Turnip Wedges with Goat Cheese

32 Buffalo Cauliflower Steaks

33 Grilled Zucchini with Basil and Orange Zest

Crispy Potato Wedges

Prep Time: 10 minutes | Cook Time: 20 minutes | Serves: 4

2 large russet potatoes, each cut into six wedges
1 tablespoon vegetable oil
Kosher salt

1 teaspoon dried oregano
2 ounces feta, crumbled

1. When ready to cook, set Traeger temperature to 475°F and preheat, lid closed for 15 minutes. 2. In a large bowl, toss the potatoes with the oil until coated. Season with salt and the oregano; toss again. 3. Put the potato wedges on the grill grate. Close the lid and cook for 20 to 25 minutes or until crispy and brown on the outside and fluffy and tender on the inside. 4. Transfer to a serving dish. Top with the feta and serve immediately.

Southern Baked Beans

Prep Time: 20 minutes | Cook Time: 2½ hours | Serves: 12

3 tablespoons extra-virgin olive oil
1-pound bacon, cut into thin slices
8 cups navy beans
4 cups beef stock
2 cups diced Roma tomatoes
1 cup dark molasses
1 cup packed dark brown sugar
1 tablespoon dried mustard

¼ teaspoon ground cloves
2 tablespoons tomato paste
2 tablespoons Worcestershire sauce
Flaked sea salt
Freshly ground black pepper
1 yellow onion, diced
1 red bell pepper, stemmed, seeded, and diced
1 green bell pepper, stemmed, seeded, and diced

1. When ready to cook, set Traeger temperature to 250°F and preheat, lid closed for 15 minutes. 2. Place a large cast iron casserole, such as a Dutch oven, on the grill grate to preheat, then pour in the olive oil and add the bacon. Cook the bacon for 30 to 45 minutes, tossing occasionally, until completely cooked. 3. In a large bowl, stir together the beans, beef stock, tomatoes, molasses, sugar, mustard, cloves, and tomato paste until blended. Stir in the Worcestershire sauce and season the mixture with salt and pepper. Set aside. 4. Add the onion, green bell pepper, and red bell pepper to the casserole. Season with salt and pepper. Toss to coat. Close the lid and cook for 30 minutes. 5. Stir the bean mixture into the casserole. Cook for 90 minutes. Remove the casserole from the grill. Season with salt and pepper to taste.

Balsamic Brussels Sprouts with Pomegranate Seeds, Walnuts, and Grapes

Prep Time: 20 minutes | Cook Time: 25 minutes | Serves: 4

12 ounces brussels sprouts, halved (quartered if large)
1 teaspoon vegetable oil
Kosher salt
Freshly ground black pepper
½ cup balsamic vinegar
¼ cup Greek yogurt

¼ cup finely chopped fresh mint
2 tablespoons water
10 grapes, cut into thin rounds
2 ounces sliced basturma or bresaola, finely chopped (optional)
⅓ cup roughly chopped toasted walnuts
¼ cup pomegranate seeds

1. When ready to cook, set Traeger temperature to 425°F and preheat, lid closed for 15 minutes. 2. In a large bowl, toss the Brussels sprouts with the oil to coat. Season with salt and pepper; toss again. Transfer to the skillet. 3. Place the skillet on the grill grate. Close the grill lid and cook for 25 to 30 minutes or until tender and browned. 4. Meanwhile, in a small saucepan, heat the vinegar over medium heat on the stove top for 8 to 9 minutes or until reduced by three-quarters. In a small bowl, stir together the yogurt, mint, and water. Season with salt. 5. Transfer the Brussels sprouts to a large serving bowl. Toss with the grapes, basturma (if using), and reduced vinegar. Top with the walnuts and pomegranate seeds. Drizzle with the mint yogurt. Serve immediately or at room temperature.

Garlic Leek and White Beans Casserole

Prep Time: 20 minutes | Cook Time: 2 hours | Serves: 8

2 tablespoons extra-virgin olive oil
4 leeks, white parts only, quartered lengthwise and thinly sliced
8 fingerling potatoes, cut lengthwise into slices
1 garlic bulb, halved
Flaked sea salt
Freshly ground black pepper

1 cup white wine
3 parsley sprigs, leaves stripped and minced
4 cups cannellini beans
1 cup chicken stock
Grated zest of 1 lemon, plus juice of 1 lemon
1 cup finely grated Gruyère cheese

1. When ready to cook, set Traeger temperature to 275°F and preheat, lid closed for 15 minutes. 2. Place a large cast iron casserole, such as a Dutch oven, on the grill grate to preheat, then pour in the olive oil. 3. Add the leeks and potatoes to the casserole. Place the garlic halves in the pot cut-side down. Season with salt and pepper. Close the lid and cook for 1 hour. 4. Stir in the white wine to deglaze the pan, scraping up any browned bits from the bottom. 5. Add the parsley, beans, chicken stock, lemon zest, and lemon juice. Season with salt and pepper. Smoke for about 1 hour more, or until your desired consistency is reached. 6. To serve, squeeze the garlic cloves from the head and add them back to the casserole. Taste and season with more salt and pepper, as needed, and top with the Gruyère cheese.

Eggplant Cucumber Salad

Prep Time: 20 minutes | Cook Time: 15 minutes | Serves: 4

1 large Italian eggplant
½ teaspoon vegetable oil
½ pint grape tomatoes, finely diced
½ green bell pepper, seeded and finely diced
1 persian cucumber, finely diced
¼ red onion, finely diced

Juice of 1 lemon
1 tablespoon extra-virgin olive oil
½ teaspoon smoked paprika
Kosher salt
Freshly ground black pepper

1. When ready to cook, set Traeger temperature to 550°F and preheat, lid closed for 15 minutes. 2. Using a fork, poke holes in several places on the eggplant. Coat with the vegetable oil. 3. Put the eggplant on the grill grate. Close the lid and cook for 15 to 20 minutes or until charred and the flesh pulls away from the skin. Transfer to a plate and refrigerate. 4. Once cool enough to handle, halve the eggplant lengthwise; scoop the flesh into a large bowl. 5. Stir in the tomatoes, bell pepper, cucumber, onion, lemon juice, olive oil, and paprika. Season with salt and pepper. Serve chilled.

Spicy Black Turtle Beans

Prep Time: 20 minutes | Cook Time: 2 hours | Serves: 8

1 tablespoon extra-virgin olive oil
1 tablespoon unsalted butter
1 yellow onion, diced
1 jalapeño pepper, trimmed, seeded, diced, plus more for additional heat
3 garlic cloves, minced

Flaked sea salt
Freshly ground black pepper
6 cups black turtle beans
3 fresh bay leaves
2 cups chicken (or vegetable) stock

1. When ready to cook, set Traeger temperature to 250°F and preheat, lid closed for 15 minutes. 2. Place a large cast iron casserole, such as a Dutch oven, on the grill grate to preheat, then pour in the olive oil and add the butter to melt. 3. Add the onion, jalapeño, and garlic to the casserole. Season with salt and pepper and toss to coat with the oil and butter. Cook for 30 minutes. 4. Using a heatproof spatula, stir in the beans, bay leaves, and chicken stock. Cook for 90 minutes, or until soft. Taste and season with more jalapeño, salt, and pepper, as needed.

Lemon Broccoli with Parmesan

Prep Time: 10 minutes | Cook Time: 15 minutes | Serves: 4

1 head broccoli, cut into florets
2 teaspoons vegetable oil
Grated zest of 1 lemon
Kosher salt

Freshly ground black pepper
¼ cup grated parmesan cheese
Extra-virgin olive oil, for serving

1. When ready to cook, set Traeger temperature to 475°F and preheat, lid closed for 15 minutes. 2. In a large bowl, toss the broccoli with the vegetable oil until coated. Add the lemon zest and season with salt and pepper; toss again. Transfer to the skillet. 3. Place the skillet on the grill grate. Close the grill lid and cook for 15 to 20 minutes or until the broccoli is tender and browned around the edges. Transfer to a serving dish. 4. Sprinkle with the Parmesan, drizzle with olive oil, and serve immediately.

Balsamic Portabello Mushroom & Cheese Panini

Prep Time: 20 minutes | Cook Time: 15 minutes | Serves: 4

Marinade:
1 cup extra-virgin olive oil
⅓ cup balsamic vinegar
2 tablespoons minced garlic
2 teaspoons dried oregano
1 teaspoon kosher salt
½ teaspoon crushed red pepper flakes

½ teaspoon freshly ground black pepper
8 portabello mushrooms, each about 4 inches in diameter, stems trimmed evenly with the bottoms
4 round crusty rolls, split
2 cups grated fontina or mozzarella cheese (7 ounces)
1 cup tightly packed baby arugula

1. Whisk the marinade ingredients. Spread the mushrooms in a single layer on a rimmed baking sheet and spoon the marinade over them. Turn to coat both sides generously. Let stand at room temperature for 30 minutes to 1 hour. 2. When ready to cook, set Traeger temperature to 400°F and preheat, lid closed for 15 minutes. 3. Place the mushrooms directly on the grill grate, smooth side facing up first, with the lid closed, cook until juicy and tender, 8 to 12 minutes, turning once or twice and brushing with the marinade left on the baking sheet. Remove from the grill. 4. Reduce the temperature of the grill to 350°F. 5. Sprinkle the bottom half of each roll with ¼ cup of the cheese. Stack 2 mushrooms on each roll, then top the mushrooms with another ¼ cup of the cheese, ¼ cup of the arugula, and the top half of the roll. Press the top of the roll firmly to compress. Place the sandwiches on the grill grate and press them down, one at a time, with a grill press or a wide, sturdy spatula. Grill until the bread is toasted and the cheese is melted, 2 to 4 minutes, turning once and pressing them flat after turning. Remove from the grill, cut in half, and serve immediately.

Asian-Spiced Bok Choy

Prep Time: 10 minutes | Cook Time: 10 minutes | Serves: 4

2 tablespoons soy sauce
2 tablespoons olive oil
1 teaspoon sesame oil
1 teaspoon minced garlic

1 teaspoon minced peeled fresh ginger
1 teaspoon white pepper
1 teaspoon Chinese five-spice powder
8 mini bok choy heads, washed and halved

1. Set Traeger temperature to 400°F and preheat, lid closed for 15 minutes. 2. In large bowl, whisk the soy sauce, olive oil, and sesame oil to combine. Add the garlic, ginger, white pepper, and five-spice powder and whisk until combined. Add the bok choy to the marinade and turn to coat. Cover and let marinate at room temperature for 15 minutes. 3. When preheating is complete, remove the bok choy from the marinade and place the bok choy halves on the grill grate. Discard the marinade. Cook, uncovered, for 10 minutes, turning every 2 to 3 minutes, until slightly translucent and there are dark brown grill marks on the leaves and stems. Serve immediately.

Grilled Corn on the Cob

4 ears corn with husks
8 tablespoons (1 stick) butter, at room temperature
4 tablespoons grated Parmesan cheese

4 teaspoons salt
2 teaspoons white pepper

1. Set Traeger temperature to 400°F and preheat, lid closed for 15 minutes. 2. Pull back the husks on each ear of corn but do not remove them from the stem. Clean off the corn silks from each ear and rinse well. Dry each ear. 3. Spread 2 tablespoons of butter over each ear, covering it completely. Sprinkle 1 tablespoon of Parmesan cheese, 1 teaspoon of salt, and ½ teaspoon of white pepper over each ear. Return the husks to their original position on each ear of corn. Remove one outer husk and fold it in half lengthwise. Tie the husk around the top end of each ear of corn and make a knot. 4. When preheating is complete, oil the grill grate and place the corn on it. Close the lid and cook for 20 to 30 minutes, turning every few minutes, until the outer husks are dry and blackened. 5. Remove from the heat and let rest for 5 minutes before serving.

Grilled Italian-Style Portabellas

Prep Time: 20 minutes | Cook Time: 10 minutes | Serves: 4

2 tablespoons olive oil
2 tablespoons balsamic vinegar
2 garlic cloves, minced
1 tablespoon dried oregano

1 teaspoon salt
1 teaspoon black pepper
4 large portabella mushroom caps

1. In a small bowl, whisk the olive oil and vinegar to blend. Add the garlic, oregano, salt, and pepper. Whisk to combine. Reserve for basting. 2. When ready to cook, set Traeger temperature to 400°F and preheat, lid closed for 15 minutes. 3. Oil the grill grate, then place the portabella caps on the grill grate. Cook, uncovered, for 10 to 15 minutes, basting and turning every 2 to 3 minutes, until the mushrooms are dark in color and slightly shriveled (or wrinkled) in appearance. Remove from the grill and serve immediately.

Asian-Inspired Coleslaw

Prep Time: 20 minutes | Cook Time: 0 minutes | Serves: 6

⅓ cup rice wine vinegar or red wine vinegar
2 tablespoons sugar
1 teaspoon dried mustard
1 tablespoon soy sauce
½ teaspoon black pepper
1 teaspoon sesame oil

¼ cup olive oil
1 head (about 2 pounds) green cabbage, shredded
3 scallions, finely chopped
1 carrot, grated
⅓ cup finely chopped fresh cilantro
½ cup dry chow mein or ramen noodles

1. In a large bowl, whisk the sugar, vinegar, dried mustard, soy sauce, and pepper until thoroughly combined. While continuing to whisk, slowly drizzle in the sesame oil until blended. Add the olive oil slowly and continue whisking until well combined. 2. Add the cabbage, scallions, carrot, and cilantro to the bowl. Toss well until combined and coated. Cover and refrigerate for 1 to 2 hours. 3. Remove the slaw from the refrigerator and add the chow mein noodles to toss just before serving.

Pico De Gallo

Prep Time: 15 minutes | Cook Time: 0 minutes | Serves: 8

12 Roma tomatoes, stemmed, quartered, and diced
1 red onion, diced
1 bunch fresh cilantro, leaves stripped and finely chopped
1 jalapeño pepper, trimmed, seeded, and finely chopped

Grated zest of 3 limes, plus juice of 3 limes
Flaked sea salt
Freshly ground black pepper
3 canned chipotle peppers in adobo sauce, finely chopped

1. In a large bowl, stir together the tomatoes, onion, cilantro, jalapeño, lime zest, and lime juice. Taste and season with salt and pepper. 2. Stir in the chipotle peppers a little bit at a time, tasting as you go, until your desired spice level is reached.

Beer Slow-Cooked Pinto Beans

Prep Time: 20 minutes | Cook Time: 3½ hours | Serves: 6

1 onion
1 jalapeño pepper
2 cups dried pinto beans, soaked overnight
3 cups water
1 (12-ounce) bottle beer (such as porter, stout, or brown ale)
2 bay leaves

1 tablespoon chili powder
2 teaspoons salt
½ teaspoon black pepper
1 teaspoon ground cumin
1 teaspoon ground coriander

1. When ready to cook, set Traeger temperature to 350°F and preheat, lid closed for 15 minutes. 2. Finely mince the onion and jalapeño, and drain and rinse the soaked beans. Transfer the onion, jalapeño, and beans to an oven-safe Dutch oven or clay pot. 3. Add the water, beer, bay leaves, chili powder, salt, and pepper. Stir to combine. Bake, with the lid closed, for 3 hours, until the beans are soft. Stir in the cumin and coriander and cook for 30 to 45 minutes more, uncovered, or until the beans have reached your desired thickness.

Grilled Beets with Goat Cheese, Arugula, and Pistachios

Prep Time: 10 minutes | Cook Time: 45 minutes | Serves: 4

6 golden or red beets, 1½–2 pounds total, leafy tops and root ends removed
Dressing:
2 tablespoons fresh lemon juice
1 tablespoon red wine vinegar
1 teaspoon honey
½ teaspoon kosher salt
½ teaspoon freshly ground black pepper

Extra-virgin olive oil

5 ounces baby arugula (about 8 cups)
4 ounces crumbled goat cheese (about 1 cup)
3 tablespoons roughly chopped fresh tarragon leaves
½ cup shelled roasted, salted pistachios

1. When ready to cook, set Traeger temperature to 400°F and preheat, lid closed for 15 minutes. 2. Scrub the beets under cold water, and then lightly brush them all over with oil. Place the beets on the grill grate, with the lid closed, grill until they are tender but not too soft when pierced with the tip of a knife, 45 minutes to 1 hour, turning once or twice. Remove from the grill and put them in a bowl. Cover with plastic wrap and let stand at room temperature until cool enough to handle. 3. Whisk the dressing ingredients. Add ¼ cup oil in a steady stream, whisking constantly to emulsify. Set aside. 4. Remove the beets from the bowl and, using a sharp paring knife, cut off the stem ends and remove the peel. Cut each beet in half horizontally, and then cut each half into quarters or eighths. Put the beets in a bowl, drizzle with ¼ cup of the dressing, and gently toss to coat. Put the arugula in another bowl, drizzle with just enough of the remaining dressing to coat the leaves very lightly, 3 to 4 tablespoons, and toss to combine. 5. Arrange the arugula on a platter or on individual plates. Spoon the beets over the arugula. Top with the goat cheese, tarragon, and pistachios. Serve immediately.

Grilled Eggplant with Sun-Dried Tomato Vinaigrette

Prep Time: 15 minutes | Cook Time: 10 minutes | Serves: 4

Vinaigrette:

4 sun-dried tomato halves packed in oil, drained and minced
2 tablespoons balsamic vinegar
1 tablespoon minced shallot
1 teaspoon dried oregano

1 teaspoon honey
Kosher salt
Freshly ground black pepper
Extra-virgin olive oil
2 globe eggplants, each about 1 pound, ends trimmed

1. When ready to cook, set Traeger temperature to 400°F and preheat, lid closed for 15 minutes. 2. Whisk the vinaigrette ingredients, including ¼ teaspoon salt and ⅛ teaspoon pepper. Add ⅓ cup oil in a steady stream, whisking constantly to emulsify. Set aside. 3. Cut the eggplants crosswise into ½-inch slices. Brush both sides of each slice with oil and season evenly with ¼ teaspoon salt and ¼ teaspoon black pepper. Place the eggplant slices on the grill grate, with the lid closed, grill until well marked and tender, 8 to 10 minutes, turning once or twice. 4. Place the slices on a platter. Immediately spoon the vinaigrette over the top. Serve warm or at room temperature.

Garlic Bok Choy with Sesame Seeds

Prep Time: 5 minutes | Cook Time: 5 minutes | Serves: 4

2½ pounds baby bok choy, quartered lengthwise
2 teaspoons vegetable oil
3 garlic cloves, grated

2 tablespoons soy sauce
2 teaspoons sesame seeds

1. When ready to cook, set Traeger temperature to 425°F and preheat, lid closed for 15 minutes. 2. In a large bowl, toss the bok choy with the oil to coat. 3. Put the bok choy on the grill grate. Close the lid and cook, turning halfway through, for about 5 minutes total or until the leaves are charred and the stems are crisp-tender. Transfer to a bowl. 4. Toss with the garlic, soy sauce, and sesame seeds. Serve immediately.

Apple-Cabbage Slaw

Prep Time: 10 minutes | Cook Time: 0 minutes | Serves: 8

6 tablespoons apple cider vinegar
2 tablespoons wildflower honey
2 tablespoons extra-virgin olive oil
2 tablespoons mayonnaise
1 tablespoon sriracha
1 tablespoon Dijon mustard
1 tablespoon celery seed

8 cups finely shredded Savoy cabbage
2 Fuji apples, cored and cut into matchsticks
2 scallions, trimmed and thinly sliced on an angle
Grated zest of 1 lemon, plus juice of 1 lemon
Flaked sea salt
Freshly ground black pepper

1. In a large bowl, whisk together the vinegar, honey, olive oil, mayonnaise, sriracha, mustard, and celery seed until smooth and combined. 2. Add the cabbage, apples, scallions, lemon zest, and lemon juice. Toss to coat well in the dressing. Cover with plastic wrap and refrigerate for 1 hour. Toss again before serving. Season with salt and pepper to taste.

Charred Asparagus with Basil-Lime Sauce

Prep Time: 15 minutes | Cook Time: 8 minutes | Serves: 6

Sauce:

1 cup mayonnaise
2 tablespoons minced fresh basil leaves
Finely grated zest of 1 lime
2 teaspoons fresh lime juice
1 garlic clove, minced or pushed through a press

⅛ teaspoon ground cayenne pepper
2 pounds asparagus
2 tablespoons extra-virgin olive oil
½ teaspoon kosher salt
½ teaspoon freshly ground black pepper

1. Whisk the sauce ingredients. Transfer to a small serving bowl and refrigerate, covered, until ready to serve. 2. When ready to cook, set Traeger temperature to 400°F and preheat, lid closed for 15 minutes. 3. Remove and discard the tough bottom of each asparagus spear by grasping each end and bending it gently until it snaps at its natural point of tenderness, usually about two-thirds of the way down the spear. Brush the asparagus with the oil and season evenly with the salt and pepper. 4. Place the asparagus directly on the grill grate. Close the lid and cook until nicely marked and crisp-tender, 6 to 8 minutes, rolling occasionally. Remove from the grill and serve warm with the sauce.

Tuscan-Style Cannellini Beans

Prep Time: 10 minutes | Cook Time: 1½ hours | Serves: 4

1¼ cups dried cannellini beans, rinsed and picked over
¼ cup extra-virgin olive oil
3 garlic cloves, chopped
2 medium tomatoes, chopped
Kosher salt

Freshly ground black pepper
5 cups low-sodium chicken broth
1 bunch fresh sage
1 bay leaf

1. In a large bowl, cover the beans with water by 2 inches; soak overnight, then drain. 2. Set Traeger temperature to 400°F and preheat, lid closed for 15 minutes. 3. Pour the oil into the Dutch oven and place on the grill grate. Once hot, add the garlic. Close the grill lid and cook for 30 seconds to 1 minute or until golden brown. 4. Add the tomatoes. Close the lid and cook for 2 to 3 minutes or until slightly softened. Season with salt and pepper. 5. Add the beans, broth, sage, and bay leaf. Cover the Dutch oven with a tight-fitting lid. Close the grill lid and cook for 1 hour 30 minutes to 1 hour 45 minutes or until the beans are tender. Season with salt and pepper. Discard the bay leaves and sage. Serve immediately.

Teriyaki Onion Pops

Prep Time: 10 minutes | Cook Time: 1½ hours | Serves: 4

2 large whole sweet onions

2 cups Kicked-Up Teriyaki Marinade

1. Peel the onions and slice each evenly into 4 thick slices, for a total of 8 slices. Leave the slices intact; do not separate them into rings. 2. Place the slices in a shallow dish or container. Pour the marinade over the onions, cover, and refrigerate for 30 minutes to 4 hours, turning the onions once. 3. Remove the onions from the refrigerator, and drain and discard the marinade. Do not rinse the onions. 4. Insert a stainless-steel skewer into the side of each onion slice, but do not push it all the way through. You want the skewers to look like onion "lollipops."5. Set Traeger temperature to 250°F and preheat, lid closed for 15 minutes. 6. Place the onions on the grill grate and smoke for 1½ hours, turning a couple of times during smoking. 7. Remove the skewers when the onions are tender and hot, and serve immediately.

Savory Jerk-Marinated Tofu

Prep Time: 30 minutes | Cook Time: 15 minutes | Serves: 2

1 (12-ounce) block extra-firm tofu
⅓ cup jerk marinade

2 tablespoons soy sauce

1. Press the tofu for 30 minutes using a heavy weight (such as a cast iron skillet). Pat dry and transfer to a shallow dish. Pour in the marinade and turn the tofu over to coat; marinate for 30 minutes at room temperature. 2. Set Traeger temperature to 400°F and preheat, lid closed for 15 minutes. 3. Put the tofu on the grill grate. Close the lid and cook for 15 to 20 minutes or until the marinade has caramelized around the edges and the tofu is heated through. Transfer to a plate. 4. Cut into ¼-inch-thick slices, drizzle with the soy sauce, and serve immediately.

Savory Cauliflower Steaks

Prep Time: 10 minutes | Cook Time: 45 minutes | Serves: 4

2 heads cauliflower, leaves removed
¼ cup olive oil
¼ cup A1 Sauce, or Heinz 57 Steak Sauce, plus more for serving

2 garlic cloves, minced
2 teaspoons salt
2 teaspoons freshly ground black pepper

1. Set Traeger temperature to 350°F and preheat, lid closed for 15 minutes. 2. Trim the base off each cauliflower. Save the excess cauliflower florets for another use. 3. Carefully slice each head of cauliflower from top to bottom through the base into 2 thick slices. 4. In a small bowl, stir together the olive oil, steak sauce, garlic, salt and pepper. Brush both sides of the "steaks" with the mixture and let them marinate on the counter for about 10 minutes to absorb the flavors. 5. Place the cauliflower directly on the grill grate. Smoke for 45 minutes to 1 hour until tender. 6. Serve with additional steak sauce.

Cheese Corn and Pepper Salad

Prep Time: 15 minutes | Cook Time: 12 minutes | Serves: 6

2 tablespoons olive oil
8 ears corn on the cob, shucked
2 jalapeño peppers
1 red bell pepper
1 red onion, thickly sliced
Kosher salt
Freshly ground black pepper

½ cup mayonnaise
½ cup sour cream
1 tablespoon chili powder
1 teaspoon garlic powder
Pinch cayenne pepper
1 cup Cotija cheese
½ cup chopped fresh cilantro

1. Set Traeger temperature to 450°F and preheat, lid closed for 15 minutes. 2. Brush olive oil on all sides of the corn, jalapeños, bell pepper, and onion. Season everything with salt and black pepper. 3. Place the corn, jalapeños, bell pepper, and onion on the grill grate and cook for 10 to 12 minutes, turning a few times. 4. Let the veggies cool after removing them from the grill. Cut the corn kernels off the cob and place in a large bowl. Remove the stems and seeds from the peppers and dice them. Dice the onion and place everything into the bowl with the corn. 5. Add the mayonnaise, sour cream, chili powder, garlic powder, cayenne pepper to taste, Cotija cheese, and cilantro. Stir to combine. Taste to adjust seasoning and add more salt and black pepper if needed.

Simple Smoked Spaghetti Squash

Prep Time: 10 minutes | Cook Time: 3 hours | Serves: 4

1 spaghetti squash, ends trimmed, halved lengthwise, seeds and pulp discarded
2 tablespoons olive oil

2 teaspoons salt
2 teaspoons freshly ground black pepper

1. When ready to cook, set Traeger temperature to 275°F and preheat, lid closed for 15 minutes. 2. Rub the cut sides of the squash generously with the olive oil and sprinkle with the salt and pepper. Place the squash, cut-sides down, on the grill grate and smoke for 2½ to 3 hours until the flesh pulls apart into strands easily. 3. Discard the skins and serve the squash as a side dish, or use in place of pasta with marinara or Alfredo sauce.

Crispy Sweet Potato Wedges

Prep Time: 10 minutes | Cook Time: 30 minutes | Serves: 4

2 sweet potatoes
2 tablespoons olive oil
1 teaspoon chili powder
1 teaspoon ground cumin

1 teaspoon ground cinnamon
Kosher salt
Freshly ground black pepper

1. Set Traeger temperature to 350°F and preheat, lid closed for 15 minutes. 2. Cut each sweet potato in half lengthwise, then cut each half into 6 wedges (for a total of 24 wedges). Brush olive oil on all sides of the wedges and sprinkle with chili powder, cumin, cinnamon, and a pinch each of salt and pepper. 3. Place the sweet potato wedges on the grill grate for 15 minutes, then flip them and cook for another 15 minutes. 4. Serve as is or with a dipping sauce of your choice.

Grilled Romaine Hearts Caesar Salad

Prep Time: 30 minutes | Cook Time: 2 minutes | Serves: 6

For the Caesar Dressing:
6 anchovy fillets packed in oil, drained and finely chopped
1 garlic clove, minced
Salt
2 large egg yolks
2 tablespoons lemon juice, plus more to taste
¾ teaspoon Dijon mustard
For the Salad:
3 or 4 romaine hearts, rinsed, dried, and halved
Avocado oil spray
Salt

1 teaspoon hot sauce
1 teaspoon Worcestershire sauce
2 tablespoons vegetable oil
½ cup extra-virgin olive oil
3 tablespoons finely grated Parmesan cheese
Pinch freshly ground black pepper

Freshly ground black pepper
4 to 6 slices Spicy Candied Bacon, crumbled
Shaved Parmesan cheese, for serving

1. To make the Caesar dressing: In a small bowl, use the back of a spoon or fork to mash the anchovies, garlic, and a pinch of salt into a paste. Work them into each other for a minute or two to incorporate. Scrape the anchovy-garlic paste into a medium bowl. Whisk in the egg yolks, lemon juice, and Dijon mustard. Add the hot sauce and Worcestershire sauce and whisk for 1 minute. Gradually whisk in the vegetable oil, then the olive oil, and continue to whisk until the dressing is thick and glossy. Add the Parmesan cheese and season with a pinch of pepper and more salt and lemon juice, if desired. Whisk again to combine, then cover and refrigerate until ready to serve. 2. To make the salad: Set Traeger temperature to 450°F and preheat, lid closed for 15 minutes. 3. Spray the cut side of each romaine heart with avocado oil, season with salt and pepper, and set aside. 4. When the grill is hot, place the romaine hearts cut-side down evenly across the grill. Cook for 1 to 2 minutes, until you see visible grill marks, making sure not to burn the lettuce. 5. When the hearts have a nice char, remove them from the grill to a serving platter. Let rest for 5 minutes. 6. To serve, top the hearts with Caesar dressing, crumbled candied bacon, and shaved Parmesan.

Eggplant Slices with Spicy Dressing

Prep Time: 10 minutes | Cook Time: 10 minutes | Serves: 4

Dressing:

1 to 2 serrano chile peppers, seeded and minced
3 tablespoons soy sauce
2 tablespoons fresh lemon juice
2 tablespoons minced yellow onion

1 tablespoon water
2 globe eggplants, each about 12 ounces
¼ cup vegetable oil
1 teaspoon garlic powder

1. Set Traeger temperature to 400°F and preheat, lid closed for 15 minutes. 2. In a small bowl, whisk together all the dressing ingredients. Set aside. 3. Remove about ½ inch from both ends of each eggplant. Cut the eggplants crosswise into ½-inch-thick slices. Lightly brush both sides of the slices with oil and evenly sprinkle them with garlic powder. 4. Grill the eggplant slices, with the lid closed, until well marked and tender, 8 to 10 minutes, turning once. Remove from the grill. 5. Arrange the eggplant slices in a single layer on a platter and immediately spoon the dressing evenly over the top. Serve warm.

Grilled Butter Carrots

Prep Time: 10 minutes | Cook Time: 10 minutes | Serves: 4

8 medium carrots, each 6 to 8 inches long and about 1-inch-wide at the stem, peeled
¼ cup (½ stick) unsalted butter
½ teaspoon red wine vinegar

¼ teaspoon freshly ground nutmeg
½ teaspoon kosher salt, divided
¼ teaspoon freshly ground black pepper, divided
1 teaspoon minced fresh Italian parsley leaves

1. Have a large bowl of ice water ready. Bring a large pot of salted water to a rolling boil. Add the carrots and cook until partially cooked but still crisp, 4 to 6 minutes. Drain the carrots and then plunge them into the ice water to stop the cooking. When the carrots are cool, drain well and set aside in a single layer on a large platter. 2. Set Traeger temperature to 500°F and preheat, lid closed for 15 minutes. 3. In a small saucepan over medium heat on the stove, melt the butter with the vinegar and nutmeg and stir to mix. Remove from the heat and brush about half of the mixture on the carrots, coating evenly. Season the carrots with half of the salt and pepper. 4. Place the carrots on the grill grate, with the lid open, grill until lightly charred with spots and stripes, 3 to 5 minutes, turning occasionally. Transfer the carrots to a clean platter. 5. Brush the carrots with the remaining butter mixture and season with the remaining salt and pepper. Garnish with the parsley and serve warm.

Cheese Potatoes

Prep Time: 15 minutes | Cook Time: 3 hours | Serves: 5

5 russet potatoes
2 tablespoons olive oil
Kosher salt
Freshly ground black pepper

1½ cups whole milk, warmed
1 stick butter, softened
2 cups shredded cheddar cheese

1. Set Traeger temperature to 250°F and preheat, lid closed for 15 minutes. 2. Brush the russet potatoes with olive oil and season all sides with salt and pepper. Place the potatoes on the grill grate and cook for 2½ hours. 3. Remove the potatoes and cut them in half lengthwise. Let them cool slightly. 4. Scoop most of the potato out of the skin with a spoon and put the potato in a large bowl. Add the milk, butter, and a pinch each of salt and pepper. Beat with a hand mixer for 1 minute. Taste to adjust the seasoning and add more salt and pepper if needed. 5. Stir in the shredded cheese, then divide this mixture evenly among the potato skins. Place them back on the Traeger for 30 minutes.

Grilled Pancetta-Wrapped Asparagus

Prep Time: 10 minutes | Cook Time: 6 minutes | Serves: 4

2 tablespoons canola oil
12 medium asparagus spears
1 tablespoon olive oil

½ teaspoon freshly ground black pepper
12 pancetta slices

1. Set Traeger temperature to 400°F and preheat, lid closed for 15 minutes. 2. Trim off the woody ends of the asparagus (about an inch) and place the spears on a plate. Drizzle the asparagus with the olive oil and toss until it is fully coated. Season the asparagus with the pepper. Wrap the middle of each spear with 1 pancetta slice. 3. Place the asparagus on the grill across the grates (so they do not fall in) or use a vegetable grill pan. Cook for about 6 minutes, uncovered, turning every minute, until the pancetta is fully cooked and the asparagus is tender. 4. Remove from the grill and serve immediately.

Balsamic Turnip Wedges with Goat Cheese

Prep Time: 30 minutes | Cook Time: 25 minutes | Serves: 6

3 or 4 turnips, peeled
2 tablespoons extra-virgin olive oil, divided
1 tablespoon Poultry and Seafood Rub, divided
Avocado oil spray

¼ cup balsamic glaze
½ cup crumbled goat cheese
3 or 4 fresh basil leaves, rolled and sliced (chiffonade)

1. Cut each turnip in half, then cut each half into thirds. Place the turnip wedges in a large bowl and drizzle with 1 tablespoon of olive oil and the rub. Toss the wedges to coat evenly. Set aside. 2. Set Traeger temperature to 400°F and preheat, lid closed for 15 minutes. 3. Place the turnip wedges on the grill grate. Close the lid and cook for 15 minutes. Open the lid, spray the wedges with avocado oil, and rotate or flip them for even cooking. Replace the lid and cook for another 10 to 15 minutes. Open the lid and check the turnips for doneness. You want them to be tender but not mushy in the center, with a nice golden, crisp exterior. 4. When the wedges are done, remove them from the grill to a serving plate and let rest for 5 minutes. 5. After resting, drizzle the wedges with the remaining 1 tablespoon of olive oil and the balsamic glaze, and sprinkle crumbled goat cheese and basil on top. Serve and enjoy!

Buffalo Cauliflower Steaks

Prep Time: 25 minutes | Cook Time: 1 hour | Serves: 6

1 head cauliflower
4 tablespoons (½ stick) salted butter
1 cup hot sauce, preferably Frank's RedHot
2 tablespoons honey

1 tablespoon Dijon mustard
Classic White BBQ Sauce, for serving
¼ cup chopped fresh parsley

1. Trim the leaves around the bottom and the stem of the cauliflower so it stands upright. Wash and pat it dry with paper towels. 2. In a saucepan over medium-high heat, melt the butter, then add the hot sauce, honey, and Dijon mustard. Reduce the heat to medium and stir to combine. When the ingredients are heated through and incorporated, remove the pan from the heat and set aside. 3. Set Traeger temperature to 325°F and preheat, lid closed for 15 minutes. 4. Make sure the cauliflower is dry, then starting at the top, brush half the butter–hot sauce mixture all over the cauliflower. 5. When the grill is ready, place the cauliflower stem-side down on the grill grate. Close the lid and cook for 30 minutes. Open the lid and flip the cauliflower, brush again with the butter–hot sauce mixture, close the lid, and cook for another 30 minutes. Open the lid, flip the cauliflower, brush with the remaining butter–hot sauce, and test for doneness using the end of an instant-read thermometer. 6. When the cauliflower is ready, remove it from the grill to a cutting board and let rest for 5 to 10 minutes. 7. To serve, slice the cauliflower into 1-inch-thick "steaks." Lay them on a serving plate, drizzle with white sauce, and top with chopped parsley.

Grilled Zucchini with Basil and Orange Zest

Prep Time: 5 minutes | Cook Time: 15 minutes | Serves: 6

6 medium zucchini (about 3½ pounds), trimmed and halved lengthwise
2 teaspoons vegetable oil
Kosher salt

Grated zest of 1 orange
15 to 20 fresh basil leaves, torn
Extra-virgin olive oil, for serving
Freshly ground black pepper

1. Set Traeger temperature to 400°F and preheat, lid closed for 15 minutes. 2. In a large bowl, toss the zucchini with the oil. Season with salt. 3. Put the zucchini on the grill grate. Close the lid and cook for 13 to 15 minutes or until tender and grill marks appear. Transfer to a serving dish. 4. Sprinkle with the orange zest and basil, then drizzle with olive oil. Season with pepper. Serve immediately.

Chapter 3 Poultry Recipes

35   Lemon-Honey Glazed Chicken Breasts

35   Smoked Chicken Gumbo with Rice

36   Spiced Citrus Duck with Plums

36   BBQ Turkey Breast

36   Tea Smoked Whole Chicken

37   Authentic Chicken Marbella

37   Grilled Chicken Breasts

37   Easy Smoked Turkey

38   Grilled Chicken Tenders

38   Ballistic BBQ Smoked Fryer Chicken

38   Chicken Tagine with Tomato-Honey Jam

39   Lime Chicken with Aji Verde

39   Creole Chicken Breasts with Black-eyed Peas Salad

40   Spicy Lemongrass Chicken with Cilantro Pesto

40   Turkey Cutlets with Cherry–Cranberry Relish

41   Jamaican Jerk Chicken Leg Quarters

41   Lime Tequila-Marinated Chicken Breasts with Cajun-Spiced Rice

41   Smoked Chicken Breasts

42   Spiced Whole Chicken

42   Salty and Sweet Turkey Legs

42   Crunchy Chicken

43   Herb-Smoked Whole Turkey

43   Maple-Dijon Chicken

43   Prosciutto Butter Grilled Chicken Thighs

44   Duck Jerky

44   Barbecued Chicken Legs

44   Turkey Noodle Soup

45   Spicy Chicken Drumsticks

45   Rosemary Roasted Chicken

45   Smoked Beer Can Chicken

46   Sweet and Spicy Cinnamon Turkey Wings

46   Garlic-Sage Turkey Cutlets with Cranberry-Apple Sauce

46   Honey-Lemon Glazed Chicken Thighs

47   Grilled Chicken Drumsticks and Peaches

47   Spiced Chicken with Orange-Chipotle Barbecue Sauce

48   Teriyaki Chicken Skewers

Lemon-Honey Glazed Chicken Breasts

Prep Time: 20 minutes | Cook Time: 2 hours 15 minutes | Serves: 4

4 boneless skinless chicken breasts
2 tablespoons extra-virgin olive oil
Flaked sea salt
Freshly ground black pepper
Grated zest of 2 lemons, plus juice of 2 lemons, plus 2 lemons,

halved, for serving
4 thyme sprigs, leaves stripped and finely chopped, plus more for garnish
¼ cup clover honey

1. Set Traeger temperature to 275°F and preheat, lid closed for 15 minutes. 2. Pat the chicken dry with a paper towel. Brush the chicken all over with the olive oil. Season all sides of the chicken with salt, pepper, lemon zest, and thyme. Arrange the chicken, breast-side up, on the grill grate, leaving space between each piece. 3. Insert a probe thermometer (if available) into the thickest part of the meat. Set the target temperature for 165°F. Close the lid and smoke for about 2 hours, or until the internal temperature reaches 165°F. 4. Squeeze the juice of the zested lemons over the chicken and drizzle with the honey. Smoke for 15 minutes more. Garnish with fresh thyme. Serve with additional lemon halves for squeezing.

Smoked Chicken Gumbo with Rice

Prep Time: 30 minutes | Cook Time: 3 hours | Serves: 8

For the Rice:
1 tablespoon unsalted butter
1 tablespoon extra-virgin olive oil
1 cup diced yellow onions
Flaked sea salt
Freshly ground black pepper
For the Gumbo:
½ cup canola oil
3 pounds bone-in skin-on chicken thighs
Flaked sea salt
Freshly ground black pepper
8 ounces andouille sausage, thinly sliced
6 thick-cut smoked bacon slices
1 cup all-purpose flour
6 garlic cloves, finely chopped
1 cup diced yellow onion

2 cups long-grain white rice, or brown rice
1 tablespoon fresh thyme leaves, stripped and finely chopped
1 fresh bay leaf
4 cups chicken (or vegetable) stock

1 cup diced celery heart
1 green bell pepper, trimmed, seeded, and diced
1-quart chicken (or vegetable) stock
12 okra, cut into ½-inch slices
6 Roma tomatoes, cored, quartered, and diced
1 tablespoon fresh thyme leaves
3 fresh or dried bay leaves
Hot sauce, for serving

To make the rice: 1. Heat a large saucepan over medium-high heat and combine the butter, olive oil, and onion. Season with salt and pepper. Sauté for about 10 minutes, until the onion is golden brown. 2. Stir in the rice, thyme, and bay leaf, stirring to coat the rice in the butter and oil. 3. Add the chicken stock. Stir gently, cover the pan, and reduce the heat to low. Cook for 45 to 60 minutes, until the liquid is absorbed.

To make the gumbo: 1. Set Traeger temperature to 275°F and preheat, lid closed for 15 minutes. 2. Place a large cast iron casserole, such as a Dutch oven on the grill grate to preheat and pour in the canola oil. 3. Pat the chicken dry with a paper towel and season both sides of the chicken with salt and pepper. Arrange the chicken on the grill grate, skin-side up, leaving space between each piece. Insert a probe thermometer (if available) into the thickest part of the meat, not touching the bone. Set the target temperature for 165°F. Smoke for about 2 hours. 4. Add the sausage and bacon to the preheated casserole. Cook for about 45 minutes, or until lightly browned and the fat renders, turning the casserole 2 or 3 times. Stir in the flour, creating a roux. 5. Add the garlic, onion, celery, and green pepper. Cook for about 20 minutes, until tender. 6. Stir in the chicken stock to deglaze the pan, scraping up any browned bits from the bottom. Add the okra, tomatoes, thyme, and bay leaves. Stir to incorporate. 7. When the chicken is fully cooked, nestle it into the casserole on top of the other ingredients. Smoke for about 1 hour more, or until the okra is tender and the liquid has reduced to your desired consistency. 8. To finish, remove the chicken from the gumbo. Debone the chicken. Remove and discard the skin. Shred the meat into bite-size pieces and return the chicken to the gumbo. Season with salt and pepper. 9. Serve with a side of rice and a good Southern hot sauce.

Spiced Citrus Duck with Plums

Prep Time: 20 minutes | Cook Time: 3-4 hours | Serves: 4

2 tablespoons canola oil
1 duck, whole
Flaked sea salt
Freshly ground black pepper
4 mandarin oranges, halved, divided
8 thyme sprigs, divided

8 blue plums, halved and pitted
8 shallots, halved
4 star anise, whole
4 cloves, whole
2 cinnamon sticks, whole
1 (750-mL) bottle sauvignon blanc

1. When ready to cook, set Traeger temperature to 275°F and preheat, lid closed for 15 minutes. Coat a roasting pan with canola oil. Set aside. 2. Season the duck all over, inside and out, with salt and pepper. Stuff the cavity with 4 orange halves and 4 thyme sprigs. Set the duck in the prepared roasting pan, breast-side up. 3. Arrange the plums, shallots, star anise, cloves, cinnamon sticks, remaining 4 orange halves, and remaining 4 thyme sprigs around the duck. 4. Pour the white wine over the ingredients surrounding the duck. Season with salt and pepper. 5. Place the roasting pan on the grill grate. Insert a probe thermometer (if available) into the thickest part of the meat, not touching the bone. Set the target temperature for 165°F. Smoke for about 2 hours, opening the smoker occasionally to spoon the rendered liquids over the entire dish. Continue to smoke for 1 to 2 hours more, or until the internal temperature reaches 165°F. 6. Remove the duck from the grill, loosely tent it with aluminum foil, and let it rest for 20 minutes. 7. Remove and discard the thyme, star anise, and cinnamon sticks. Serve the duck with a side of the plums and shallots.

BBQ Turkey Breast

Prep Time: 5 minutes | Cook Time: 1 hour | Serves: 4

2 tablespoons canola oil
2 tablespoons freshly ground black pepper
4 teaspoons kosher salt

3 pounds boneless, skinless turkey breast
2 teaspoons mayonnaise
4 tablespoons (½ stick) cold unsalted butter, cut into 4 pieces

1. Set Traeger temperature to 400°F and preheat, lid closed for 15 minutes. 2. In a small bowl, stir together the pepper and salt. Rub the turkey breast with the mayonnaise (this acts as a binder) and season it generously with the pepper-salt mixture. 3. Place the turkey, skin-side down on the grill grate, close the lid and cook for 20 minutes. Flip the turkey, close the lid, and cook the meat for 20 minutes more, until the internal temperature reaches 150°F. 4. Tear a piece of aluminum foil into a by 12-inch square and place the butter pieces on the foil. Remove the turkey from the grill and place it on the butter. Wrap and seal the foil around the meat to make an airtight packet and put the packet on the grill grate for 10 minutes. Flip the foil packet and cook for 10 minutes more until the meat's internal temperature reaches 165°F. 5. Remove the packet from the grill and let it rest for 10 minutes before carefully opening the foil. Slice the turkey and serve.

Tea Smoked Whole Chicken

Prep Time: 25 minutes | Cook Time: 4 hours | Serves: 8

1 whole chicken
2 cups Tea Injectable (using Not-Just-for-Pork Rub)
2 tablespoons olive oil

1 batch Chicken Rub
2 tablespoons butter, melted

1. Set Traeger temperature to 180°F and preheat, lid closed for 15 minutes. 2. Inject the chicken throughout with the tea injectable. 3. Coat the chicken all over with olive oil and season it with the rub. Using your hands, work the rub into the meat. 4. Place the chicken directly on the grill grate and smoke for 3 hours. 5. Baste the chicken with the butter and increase the grill's temperature to 375°F. Continue to cook the chicken until its internal temperature reaches 170°F. 6. Remove the chicken from the grill and let it rest for 10 minutes, before carving and serving.

Authentic Chicken Marbella

Prep Time: 30 minutes | Cook Time: 3 hours | Serves: 8

½ cup red wine vinegar
¼ cup extra-virgin olive oil
1 cup dried pitted prunes
½ cup capers
½ cup pitted green olives
6 garlic cloves, minced
¼ cup fresh oregano leaves, finely chopped
3 fresh or dried bay leaves

2 (3- to 4-pound) chickens, whole, separated into breasts, legs, thighs, and wings
Flaked sea salt
Freshly ground black pepper
2 cups sauvignon blanc or Riesling
½ cup packed light brown sugar
¼ cup fresh flat-leaf parsley leaves, finely chopped

1. In a large bowl, whisk together the vinegar, olive oil, prunes, capers, olives, garlic, oregano, and bay leaves. Add the chicken and turn to coat. Cover the bowl with plastic wrap and refrigerate for 24 hours, turning the chicken 2 or 3 times. 2. When ready to cook, set Traeger temperature to 275°F and preheat, lid closed for 15 minutes. 3. Place a large roasting pan on a smoking rack to preheat. 4. Strain the chicken and pat it dry, reserving the marinade in the refrigerator. Season the chicken on both sides with salt and pepper. Arrange the chicken on the grill grate, skin-side up, leaving space between each piece. Insert a probe thermometer (if available) into the thickest part of the meat, not touching the bone. Set the target temperature for 165°F. Smoke for about 2 hours, or until the internal temperature reaches 165°F. 5. Arrange the chicken in one layer in the roasting pan and coat it evenly with the reserved marinade. 6. Pour in the white wine and sprinkle the chicken evenly with the sugar. Return the chicken to the grill for 60 to 90 minutes, basting it occasionally, until the sauce reaches the desired consistency. 7. Serve topped with fresh parsley and the prune and olive pan sauce. Remove and discard the bay leaves.

Grilled Chicken Breasts

Prep Time: 10 minutes | Cook Time: 45 minutes | Serves: 4

2 (1-pound) bone-in, skin-on chicken breasts

1 batch Chicken Rub

1. Set Traeger temperature to 350°F and preheat, lid closed for 15 minutes. 2. Season the chicken breasts all over with the rub. Using your hands, work the rub into the meat. 3. Place the breasts directly on the grill grate and smoke until their internal temperature reaches 170°F, about 45 minutes. Remove the breasts from the grill and serve immediately.

Easy Smoked Turkey

Prep Time: 15 minutes | Cook Time: 4 hours | Serves: 10

1 whole turkey
2 tablespoons olive oil

2 batches Chicken Rub (you may have some left over)

1. Set Traeger temperature to 180°F and preheat, lid closed for 15 minutes. 2. Coat the turkey with olive oil and season it with the rub. Using your hands, work the rub into the meat and skin. 3. Place the turkey directly on the grill grate and smoke for 3 hours. 4. Increase the grill's temperature to 375°F and continue to cook until the turkey's internal temperature reaches 170°F. 5. Remove the turkey from the grill and let it rest for 10 minutes, before carving and serving.

Grilled Chicken Tenders

Prep Time: 10 minutes | Cook Time: 1½ hours | Serves: 4

1 pound boneless, skinless chicken breast tenders   1 batch Chicken Rub

1. Set Traeger temperature to 180°F and preheat, lid closed for 15 minutes. 2. Season the chicken tenders with the rub. Using your hands, work the rub into the meat. 3. Place the tenders directly on the grill grate and smoke for 1 hour. 4. Increase the grill's temperature to 300°F and continue to cook until the tenders' internal temperature reaches 170°F. Remove the tenders from the grill and serve immediately.

Ballistic BBQ Smoked Fryer Chicken

Prep Time: 30 minutes | Cook Time: 3 hours | Serves: 6

1 fryer chicken, cut in half or into pieces   Freshly ground black pepper
Kosher salt   1½ cups Ballistic BBQ Sauce

1. Set Traeger temperature to 250°F and preheat, lid closed for 15 minutes. 2. Season all sides of the chicken with a few pinches of salt and pepper. 3. Insert the probe into the thickest part of the chicken, avoiding the bone. Place the chicken on the grill grate and close the lid. Cook until the chicken reaches 150°F at the thigh, then open the dampers (on a charcoal or wood-burning cooker) and bring the grill temperature up to 300°F. 4. When the internal temperature of the chicken reaches 170°F, baste the chicken with the glaze and close the lid. 5. Once the internal temperature of the chicken reaches 175°F, remove it from the grill and serve.

Chicken Tagine with Tomato-Honey Jam

Prep Time: 20 minutes | Cook Time: 1 hour | Serves: 8

6 pounds ripe heirloom tomatoes, seeded and coarsely chopped   1 teaspoon ground cinnamon
½ cup sugar   ½ teaspoon ground coriander
¼ cup honey   ¼ teaspoon ground ginger
6 pounds chicken parts, a mixture of breasts and thighs   ¼ teaspoon crumbled saffron threads placed in ¼ cup warm water
2 cups finely chopped onions   1 cup low-sodium chicken broth
¼ cup extra-virgin olive oil   ½ cup unsalted roasted shelled pistachios
1 tablespoon finely chopped garlic   3 cups cooked basmati rice
1 teaspoon ground cumin

1. The day before you plan to make this dish, make the jam. In a large skillet, combine the tomatoes, sugar, and honey and bring to a boil. Reduce the heat to low and cook, uncovered, stirring occasionally, until the mixture is thickened and jamlike, about 1 hour. Let cool completely, then refrigerate in an airtight container until ready to serve; it will keep for up to a week. 2. Set Traeger temperature to 375°F and preheat, lid closed for 15 minutes. 3. While the grill comes to temperature, toss the chicken, onions, oil, and garlic together in a large bowl. Sprinkle with the spices and toss to coat. Add the saffron mixture and toss one more time. Arrange the chicken mixture in the bottom of a tagine or cast-iron Dutch oven. Pour in the broth, cover, and place on the grill. Close the lid and cook until the internal temperature of the thighs is 165°F, about 1 hour. 4. Remove the tagine from the grill and place on a trivet at your table. Open the lid (be careful of the steam that will come out) and spoon some of the tomato jam over each piece of chicken. Sprinkle with the pistachios and serve immediately with basmati rice.

Lime Chicken with Aji Verde

Prep Time: 20 minutes | Cook Time: 3 hours | Serves: 4

For the Chicken:
Juice of 2 limes
3 garlic cloves, minced
3 tablespoons olive oil
1 tablespoon white vinegar
1 tablespoon aji amarillo paste
1 tablespoon aji panca paste
For the Aji Verde:
1 cup chopped fresh cilantro
⅔ cup mayonnaise
1½ tablespoons freshly squeezed lime juice
1 tablespoon aji amarillo paste

1 tablespoon soy sauce
1½ teaspoons salt
2 teaspoons ground cumin
1½ teaspoons freshly ground black pepper
½ teaspoon smoked paprika
1 (3-pound) whole chicken

1 garlic clove
¼ teaspoon onion powder
¼ teaspoon salt

To make the chicken: 1. Combine the lime juice, garlic, olive oil, white vinegar, aji amarillo paste, aji panca paste, soy sauce, salt, cumin, black pepper, and smoked paprika in a blender or food processor. Puree, then set aside. 2. Pat the chicken dry with paper towels. Trim away any loose skin. Rub the marinade all over the chicken, including under the breast skin and inside the cavity. Place into a glass baking dish and cover tightly with plastic wrap. Marinate in the refrigerator for 8 to 24 hours. 3. Set Traeger temperature to 250°F and preheat, lid closed for 15 minutes. 4. Place the marinated chicken on the grill grate, close the lid, and cook for 3 to 4 hours, or until the internal temperature of the thigh meat reaches 195°F. If you'd like some crispness on the skin, increase the heat of your cooker to 350°F and broil the chicken for the last 30 minutes of cook time. 5. Once cooked, remove, place on a clean cutting board, and loosely tent with aluminum foil. Let it rest for 10 to 15 minutes before carving.

To make the aji verde: Place the cilantro, mayonnaise, lime juice, aji amarillo paste, garlic, onion powder, and salt into a food processor or blender. Puree the mixture and serve with the carved chicken.

Creole Chicken Breasts with Black-eyed Peas Salad

Prep Time: 25 minutes | Cook Time: 35 minutes | Serves: 4

Dressing:
4 ½ tablespoons extra-virgin olive oil
3 tablespoons cider vinegar
Salad:
2 cans (each 15 ounces) black-eyed peas, rinsed and drained
10 ounces grape tomatoes, each cut in half (about 2 cups)
4 ounces smoked ham, cut into ⅓-inch cubes
⅓ cup finely chopped celery
Kosher salt
Freshly ground black pepper
4 chicken breast halves (with bone and skin), each 10–12 ounces

1 tablespoon creole mustard
1 tablespoon honey

1 tablespoon extra-virgin olive oil
2 ½ teaspoons Cajun seasoning
¼ cup plus 2 tablespoons creole mustard
1 tablespoon honey
2 teaspoons minced fresh thyme leaves
4 cups loosely packed watercress sprigs, thick stems trimmed (about 1 bunch)

1. In a large bowl, whisk the dressing ingredients. Add the salad ingredients and toss to coat with the dressing. Season with salt and pepper. Cover and refrigerate until ready to serve. 2. Set Traeger temperature to 400°F and preheat, lid closed for 15 minutes. 3. Brush the chicken breasts on both sides with the oil and season evenly with the Cajun seasoning, 1½ teaspoons salt, and 1 teaspoon pepper. 4. Whisk the creole mustard and the honey together. Place close by the grill. 5. Grill the chicken, bone side down, on the grill grate, with the lid closed, until the meat is almost firm to the touch, 25 to 35 minutes. Brush the honey mustard evenly over the chicken. Continue to grill until the juices run clear and the meat is no longer pink at the bone, 5 to 10 minutes more, brushing occasionally with the remaining honey mustard. Remove from the grill and season the skin side of the chicken evenly with the thyme. Let the chicken rest for 3 to 5 minutes. 6. Add the watercress to the salad and toss gently to combine. Serve the chicken warm with the salad.

Spicy Lemongrass Chicken with Cilantro Pesto

Prep Time: 20 minutes | Cook Time: 10 minutes | Serves: 4

Marinade:

2 stalks lemongrass
¼ cup cider vinegar
¼ cup peanut oil
2 scallions, ends trimmed and roughly chopped
2 tablespoons finely chopped fresh cilantro leaves
1 tablespoon peeled, minced fresh ginger

1 teaspoon minced garlic
Kosher salt
Freshly ground black pepper
4 boneless chicken breast halves (with or without skin), each about 6 ounces

Pesto:

2 cups coarsely chopped fresh cilantro leaves
¾ cup loosely packed fresh Italian parsley leaves
¼ cup plus 1 tablespoon extra-virgin olive oil
1 tablespoon peeled, coarsely chopped fresh ginger
1 garlic clove, coarsely chopped

⅛ teaspoon ground cayenne pepper
½ cup panko bread crumbs
2 tablespoons all-purpose flour
1 teaspoon crushed red pepper flakes
Olive oil cooking spray

1. Peel away the dry outer layers of the lemongrass stalks, trim the ends, and mince the tender parts; you should have about ¼ cup. In a large nonreactive bowl whisk the lemongrass with the remaining marinade ingredients, including ¾ teaspoon salt and ½ teaspoon pepper. Place the chicken in the bowl with the marinade and turn to coat. Cover and refrigerate for 1 to 6 hours, turning occasionally. 2. In a food processor, combine the pesto ingredients, including ½ teaspoon salt and ¼ teaspoon pepper. Puree until fairly smooth. 3. Set Traeger temperature to 400°F and preheat, lid closed for 15 minutes. 4. Remove the chicken from the bowl and discard the marinade. Using paper towels, blot the chicken mostly dry, leaving some of the solid bits clinging to the chicken. In a shallow dish stir the panko with the flour, red pepper flakes, and ¼ teaspoon salt. Coat the chicken with the mixture, pressing lightly so that the mixture adheres. Lightly spray the chicken all over with oil. 5. Grill the chicken, smooth (skin) side down first, on the grill grate, with the lid closed, until the meat is firm to the touch and opaque all the way to the center, 8 to 12 minutes, turning once. Remove from the grill and let rest for 3 to 5 minutes. Serve warm with the pesto.

Turkey Cutlets with Cherry-Cranberry Relish

Prep Time: 15 minutes | Cook Time: 7 minutes | Serves: 6

Marinade:

¼ cup extra-virgin olive oil
1 tablespoon Dijon mustard
1 tablespoon chopped fresh rosemary leaves
3 large garlic cloves, finely chopped

1 teaspoon kosher salt
¼ teaspoon freshly ground black pepper
8 turkey cutlets, each about 4 ounces and ¾ inch thick

Relish:

2 cups fresh or frozen cranberries
1 cup 100% cranberry juice (no sugar added)
⅓ cup packed golden brown sugar

¼ cup dried tart cherries, roughly chopped
¼ teaspoon kosher salt

1. In a large bowl, whisk the marinade ingredients. Place the cutlets in the bowl and turn to coat. Cover and refrigerate for 1 to 4 hours. 2. Set Traeger temperature to 400°F and preheat, lid closed for 15 minutes. 3. In a medium saucepan over high heat, combine the relish ingredients and bring to a boil. Lower the heat to a simmer and cook until the cranberries are soft, 4 to 6 minutes, stirring and crushing the cranberries against the side of the saucepan often. Remove the saucepan from the heat, transfer the relish to a bowl, and let cool to room temperature. 4. Place the cutlets on the grill grate, with the lid closed, until the meat is firm to the touch and no longer pink in the center, 5 to 7 minutes, turning once after 3 to 4 minutes. Remove from the grill and serve warm with the relish.

Jamaican Jerk Chicken Leg Quarters

Prep Time: 15 minutes | Cook Time: 1 hour | Serves: 4

4 chicken leg quarters, scored
¼ cup canola oil

½ cup Jamaican Jerk Paste

1. Set Traeger temperature to 275°F and preheat, lid closed for 15 minutes. 2. Brush the chicken with canola oil, then brush 6 tablespoons of the Jerk paste on and under the skin. Reserve the remaining 2 tablespoons of paste for basting. 3. Arrange the chicken on the grill, close the lid, and smoke for 1 hour to 1 hour 30 minutes, or until a meat thermometer inserted in the thickest part of the thigh reads 165°F. 4. Let the meat rest for 5 minutes and baste with the reserved jerk paste prior to serving.

Lime Tequila-Marinated Chicken Breasts with Cajun-Spiced Rice

Prep Time: 30 minutes | Cook Time: 30 minutes | Serves: 4

Marinade:
¼ cup gold tequila
¼ cup fresh lime juice
1 tablespoon packed golden brown sugar
2 teaspoons Dijon mustard
2 teaspoons ancho chile powder
2 garlic cloves, smashed

1 teaspoon ground cumin
1 teaspoon freshly ground black pepper
Extra-virgin olive oil
Kosher salt
4 boneless chicken breast halves (with skin), each about 6 ounces

Rice:
1 tablespoon unsalted butter
¼ cup finely chopped yellow onion
1 garlic clove, minced or pushed through a press
1 teaspoon paprika
1 teaspoon dried oregano

¼ teaspoon ground cayenne pepper
1½ cups long-grain white rice
2¼ cups low-sodium chicken broth
¼ cup thinly sliced scallions, ends trimmed

1. Whisk the marinade ingredients, including 1 tablespoon oil and 1 teaspoon salt. Place the chicken in a large resealable plastic bag and pour in the marinade. Press the air out of the bag and seal tightly. Turn the bag to distribute the marinade, place in a bowl, and refrigerate for 4 to 8 hours. 2. In a medium saucepan over medium heat, warm the butter and 1 tablespoon oil. Add the onion and the garlic and sauté until the onion softens and begins to turn golden brown, about 3 minutes. Add the paprika, oregano, cayenne pepper, and 1 teaspoon salt and sauté until fragrant, about 30 seconds. Add the rice and stir until coated in the oil, about 1 minute. Add the broth and bring to a boil. Cover the pan and reduce the heat to low. Simmer until all of the liquid is absorbed, 20 to 25 minutes. Remove from the heat, fluff the rice with a fork, and stir in the scallions. Cover and keep warm. 3. Set Traeger temperature to 400°F and preheat, lid closed for 15 minutes. 4. Remove the chicken from the bag and discard the marinade. Place the chicken, skin side up first, on the grill grate, with the lid closed, until the meat is firm to the touch and no longer pink in the center, 8 to 12 minutes, turning once after 7 to 9 minutes. Remove from the grill and let rest for 3 to 5 minutes. Serve warm with the rice.

Smoked Chicken Breasts

Prep Time: 10 minutes | Cook Time: 1½ hours | Serves: 4

2½ pounds boneless, skinless chicken breasts
Salt

Freshly ground black pepper

1. Set Traeger temperature to 180°F and preheat, lid closed for 15 minutes. 2. Season the chicken breasts all over with salt and pepper. 3. Place the breasts directly on the grill grate and smoke for 1 hour. 4. Increase the grill's temperature to 325°F and continue to cook until the chicken's internal temperature reaches 170°F. Remove the breasts from the grill and serve immediately.

Spiced Whole Chicken

Prep Time: 20 minutes | Cook Time: 3 hours | Serves: 8

2 (3½- to 4-pound) whole chickens
2 tablespoons vegetable oil
⅓ cup paprika
¼ cup chili powder
1 tablespoon salt
1 tablespoon onion powder

2 teaspoons ground cumin
2 teaspoons dry mustard
2 teaspoons granulated garlic
2 teaspoons freshly ground black pepper
2 teaspoons dried parsley
1 teaspoon dried thyme

1. Set Traeger temperature to 250°F and preheat, lid closed for 15 minutes. 2. Trim away any excess skin, blot chickens dry with paper towels, and brush them all over with vegetable oil. 3. Combine the paprika, chili powder, salt, onion powder, cumin, dry mustard, granulated garlic, black pepper, parsley, and thyme in a small bowl. Divide the mixture in half, and use one half to season each chicken. Massage the rub under the breast skin and inside the cavity as well. 4. Place chickens on the grill grate, close the lid, and cook for 3 to 4 hours. It takes roughly 45 minutes per pound to smoke a chicken. Once the chickens reach 195°F in the thigh area and 185°F in the breast area, they are done. 5. Remove the chickens from your grill and let them rest for 10 minutes before carving and serving. Use heat-resistant food-safe gloves if you are planning on pulling the chicken.

Salty and Sweet Turkey Legs

Prep Time: 10 minutes | Cook Time: 4 hours | Serves: 4

1 gallon hot water
1 cup curing salt (such as Morton Tender Quick)
¼ cup packed light brown sugar
1 teaspoon freshly ground black pepper
1 teaspoon ground cloves

1 bay leaf
2 teaspoons liquid smoke
4 turkey legs
Mandarin Glaze, for serving

1. In a large container with a lid, stir together the water, curing salt, brown sugar, pepper, cloves, bay leaf, and liquid smoke until the salt and sugar are dissolved; let come to room temperature. 2. Submerge the turkey legs in the seasoned brine, cover, and refrigerate overnight. 3. When ready to cook, set Traeger temperature to 225°F and preheat, lid closed for 15 minutes. 4. Remove the turkey legs from the brine and rinse them; discard the brine. 5. Arrange the turkey legs on the grill, close the lid, and smoke for 4 to 5 hours, or until dark brown and a meat thermometer inserted in the thickest part of the meat reads 165°F. 6. Serve with Mandarin Glaze on the side or drizzled over the turkey legs.

Crunchy Chicken

Prep Time: 30 minutes | Cook Time: 55 minutes | Serves: 6

1 egg, beaten
½ cup milk
1 cup all-purpose flour
2 tablespoons salt
1 tablespoon freshly ground black pepper
2 teaspoons freshly ground white pepper

2 teaspoons cayenne pepper
2 teaspoons garlic powder
2 teaspoons onion powder
1 teaspoon smoked paprika
8 tablespoons (1 stick) unsalted butter, melted
1 whole chicken, cut up into pieces

1. Set Traeger temperature to 375°F and preheat, lid closed for 15 minutes. 2. In a medium bowl, combine the beaten egg with the milk and set aside. 3. In a separate medium bowl, stir together the flour, salt, black pepper, white pepper, cayenne, garlic powder, onion powder, and smoked paprika. 4. Line the bottom and sides of a high-sided metal baking pan with aluminum foil to ease cleanup. 5. Pour the melted butter into the prepared pan. 6. Dip the chicken pieces one at a time in the egg mixture, and then coat well with the seasoned flour. Transfer to the baking pan. 7. Smoke the chicken in the pan of butter on the grill, with the lid closed, for 25 minutes, then reduce the heat to 325°F and turn the chicken pieces over. 8. Continue smoking with the lid closed for about 30 minutes, or until a meat thermometer inserted in the thickest part of each chicken piece reads 165°F. 9. Serve immediately.

Herb-Smoked Whole Turkey

Prep Time: 10 minutes | Cook Time: 5 hours | Serves: 8

1 (10- to 12-pound) turkey, giblets removed
Extra-virgin olive oil, for rubbing
¼ cup poultry seasoning
8 tablespoons (1 stick) unsalted butter, melted

½ cup apple juice
2 teaspoons dried sage
2 teaspoons dried thyme

1. Set Traeger temperature to 250°F and preheat, lid closed for 15 minutes. 2. Rub the turkey with oil and season with the poultry seasoning inside and out, getting under the skin. 3. In a bowl, combine the melted butter, apple juice, sage, and thyme to use for basting. 4. Put the turkey in a roasting pan, place on the grill, close the lid, and grill for 5 to 6 hours, basting every hour, until the skin is brown and crispy, or until a meat thermometer inserted in the thickest part of the thigh reads 165°F. 5. Let the bird rest for 15 to 20 minutes before carving.

Maple-Dijon Chicken

Prep Time: 15 minutes | Cook Time: 16 minutes | Serves: 4

4 (6-ounce) boneless, skinless chicken breasts
½ cup maple syrup
⅓ cup course-ground Dijon mustard

3 garlic cloves, minced
2 tablespoons canola oil

1. Working with one chicken breast at a time, place it inside a gallon-size zip-top bag and seal the bag while pressing out any air. Using the flat side of a meat mallet or tenderizer, gently pound the chicken until it is completely flat and roughly ½ inch thick. Remove the chicken breast from the bag and repeat the process with the remaining breasts, then return them all to the zip-top bag. (If the bag has any holes in it, use a new bag for this step.) 2. In a small bowl, whisk together the maple syrup, mustard, and garlic. Pour half the maple syrup mixture into the bag with the chicken and seal the bag while pressing out any air. Thoroughly massage the mixture onto the chicken. 3. Set Traeger temperature to 400°F and preheat, lid closed for 15 minutes. 4. Place the chicken on the grill and cook it for 7 to 8 minutes. Flip the chicken and cook for 7 to 8 minutes more, until it reaches an internal temperature of 165°F. 5. Remove the chicken from the grill and cover loosely with aluminum foil. Let it rest for 5 minutes. Slice the chicken before serving.

Prosciutto Butter Grilled Chicken Thighs

Prep Time: 20 minutes | Cook Time: 24 minutes | Serves: 6

Butter:
¼ cup (½ stick) unsalted butter, softened
1-ounce prosciutto, very finely chopped
1 medium shallot, minced
1 tablespoon finely chopped fresh basil leaves
1 tablespoon freshly grated Parmigiano-Reggiano® cheese
¼ teaspoon kosher salt

¼ teaspoon freshly ground black pepper
8 bone-in, skin-on chicken thighs, each 5 to 6 ounces, trimmed of excess fat and skin
½ teaspoon kosher salt
¼ teaspoon freshly ground black pepper

1. In a small bowl combine all the butter ingredients and mix together with a fork. Divide the butter into eight equal portions. 2. Set Traeger temperature to 450°F and preheat, lid closed for 15 minutes. 3. Pat the chicken thighs dry with paper towels. Using your fingertips, gently loosen the skin on the thighs, being careful not to separate the skin completely from the meat. Lift the skin up and place a portion of the butter underneath. Smooth the skin over the butter and massage gently to spread the butter evenly over the meat. Season the thighs on both sides with the salt and pepper. 4. Place the thighs, skin side up first on the grill grate, with the lid closed. Cook until sizzling, slightly firm, and lightly marked on the underside, 18 to 20 minutes. Turn the thighs over and cook until the juices run clear, the skin is blistered and crisp, and the meat is no longer pink at the bone, 2 to 4 minutes more. Remove the thighs from the grill, let rest for 3 to 5 minutes, and then serve warm.

Duck Jerky

Prep Time: 1 hour | Cook Time: 5 hours | Serves: 8

1 whole duck, skin removed   1 batch Chicken Rub

1. Set Traeger temperature to 180°F and preheat, lid closed for 15 minutes. 2. Remove the duck meat from the bones and cut the meat into pieces of your desired size. 3. Season the duck pieces with the rub and use your hands to work the rub into the meat. 4. Place the duck pieces directly on the grill grate and smoke at 180°F for 5 or 6 hours, until the jerky is dried but still bendable. Remove and serve or refrigerate in an airtight container for up to 2 weeks.

Barbecued Chicken Legs

Prep Time: 30 minutes | Cook Time: 40 minutes | Serves: 4

Sauce:
2 tablespoons extra-virgin olive oil
½ cup finely chopped yellow onion
2 teaspoons minced garlic
1 cup ketchup
Rub:
2 teaspoons smoked paprika
2 teaspoons kosher salt
Finely grated zest of 1 lemon
½ teaspoon garlic powder

½ cup lemon-lime carbonated beverage (not diet)
¼ cup fresh lemon juice
¼ cup packed light brown sugar
2 tablespoons whole-grain mustard

½ teaspoon freshly ground black pepper
4 whole chicken legs, each 10 to 12 ounces, trimmed of excess fat and skin and cut into thighs and drumsticks

1. In a saucepan over medium heat, warm the oil. Add the onion and garlic and cook until golden, about 10 minutes, stirring often. Stir in all the remaining sauce ingredients and bring to a simmer. Turn down the heat to low and cook until the sauce is slightly thickened, 10 to 15 minutes, stirring often. 2. Set Traeger temperature to 400°F and preheat, lid closed for 15 minutes. 3. In a small bowl combine all the rub ingredients and mix well. Season the chicken pieces all over with the rub. 4. Grill the chicken, skin side down first, with the lid closed, until golden brown, 8 to 10 minutes, turning occasionally. Brush the chicken with a thin layer of the sauce and continue to cook, with the lid closed, until the juices run clear and the meat is no longer pink at the bone, about 30 minutes more, turning and brushing occasionally with the sauce. Remove the chicken from the grill and let rest for 3 to 5 minutes. 5. Serve the chicken warm with the remaining sauce on the side.

Turkey Noodle Soup

Prep Time: 15 minutes | Cook Time: 5 hours | Serves: 10

1 whole Smoked Turkey carcass
4 cups water
Salt
Freshly ground black pepper
½ medium white onion, diced

3 garlic cloves, minced
2 carrots, sliced
2 celery stalks, sliced
1 cup bowtie noodles

1. Set Traeger temperature to 400°F and preheat, lid closed for 15 minutes. 2. In a cast-iron Dutch oven, combine the turkey carcass and water and season it with salt and pepper. Place the pot directly on the grill grate and bring the mixture to a boil. Cover the pot and boil the carcass for 3 or 4 hours, or until the meat is easily removed from the bones. 3. Remove the pot from the grill, remove the meat from the bones, and discard the bones. Return the meat to the soup pot and stir in the onion, garlic, carrots, and celery. Cover the pot, return it to the grill, and boil the soup for about 1 hour, until the vegetables soften. 4. Stir in the noodles. Decrease the grill's temperature to 180°F and smoke the soup, uncovered, until the noodles are soft. Taste and season with more salt and pepper, as desired.

Spicy Chicken Drumsticks

Prep Time: 10 minutes | Cook Time: 20 minutes | Serves: 4

1-pound chicken drumsticks
2 tablespoons olive oil

Spicy Rub

1. Set Traeger temperature to 400°F and preheat, lid closed for 15 minutes. 2. Rub drumsticks with the olive oil and liberally season with the rub. 3. Place the drumsticks on the grill grate, close the lid, and cook for about 20 minutes, or until the internal temperature reaches 170°F. 4. Remove the drumsticks from the grill and serve immediately.

Rosemary Roasted Chicken

Prep Time: 15 minutes | Cook Time: 50 minutes | Serves: 4

Marinade:
2 tablespoons extra-virgin olive oil
1 tablespoon Dijon mustard
1 tablespoon Worcestershire sauce
1 tablespoon cider vinegar
1 tablespoon finely chopped fresh rosemary leaves

½ teaspoon kosher salt
¼ teaspoon freshly ground black pepper
1 whole chicken, about 4 pounds, neck, giblets, wing tips, and any excess fat removed

1. In a small bowl whisk together all the marinade ingredients. 2. Cut the chicken into six pieces: two breast halves, two whole legs (thigh and drumstick), and two wings. Brush each chicken piece on both sides with the marinade. If you have time, marinate the chicken in the refrigerator for up to 4 hours. If not, you can roast the chicken right away. 3. Set Traeger temperature to 400°F and preheat, lid closed for 15 minutes. 4. Grill the chicken pieces, skin side down, with the lid closed, until fully cooked, turning once or twice. The chicken breasts and wing pieces will take 30 to 40 minutes and the whole chicken legs will take 40 to 50 minutes. Remove from the grill and let rest for 3 to 5 minutes, then serve warm.

Smoked Beer Can Chicken

Prep Time: 15 minutes | Cook Time: 1½ hours | Serves: 4

2 tablespoons kosher salt
1 whole chicken, 4 to 5 pounds, neck, giblets, and any excess fat
Rub:
2 teaspoons onion powder
2 teaspoons paprika
1 teaspoon packed light brown sugar
½ teaspoon freshly ground black pepper

removed

1 tablespoon extra-virgin olive oil
Extra-virgin olive oil
1 can (12 ounces) beer, at room temperature

1. Sprinkle the salt over the meaty parts of the chicken and inside the cavity. Cover with plastic wrap and refrigerate for 2 hours. 2. In a bowl, combine all the rub ingredients and mix well. 3. Set Traeger temperature to 400°F and preheat, lid closed for 15 minutes. 4. Rinse the chicken with cold water, then pat dry with paper towels. Brush the chicken all over with oil and season all over, including inside the cavity, with the rub. Fold the wing tips behind the back. 5. Open the beer and pour out about two-thirds of it. Using a church key–style can opener, make two additional holes in the top of the can. Place the can on a solid surface and then carefully position the chicken over the can. 6. Transfer the chicken-on-a-can to the grill, close the lid and cook the chicken until the juices run clear when a thigh is pierced in the thickest part, or an instant-read thermometer inserted into the thickest part of the thigh (not touching the bone) registers 160° to 165°F, 1¼ to 1½ hours. 7. Carefully remove the chicken-on-a-can from the grill (do not spill the contents of the beer can, which will be very hot) and stand it on a heatproof surface. Let the chicken rest for 10 to 15 minutes (the internal temperature will rise 5 to 10 degrees during this time) before lifting it from the beer can and carving it into serving pieces. Serve warm.

Sweet and Spicy Cinnamon Turkey Wings

Prep Time: 10 minutes | Cook Time: 1 hour | Serves: 2

4 turkey wings

1 batch Sweet and Spicy Cinnamon Rub

1. Set Traeger temperature to 180°F and preheat, lid closed for 15 minutes. 2. Using your hands, work the rub into the turkey wings, coating them completely. 3. Place the wings directly on the grill grate and cook for 30 minutes. 4. Increase the grill's temperature to 325°F and continue to cook until the turkey's internal temperature reaches 170°F. Remove the wings from the grill and serve immediately.

Garlic-Sage Turkey Cutlets with Cranberry-Apple Sauce

Prep Time: 15 minutes | Cook Time: 6 minutes | Serves: 6

3 tablespoons extra-virgin olive oil
1 tablespoon minced fresh sage leaves
2 teaspoons minced garlic
Sauce:
1 Granny Smith apple, peeled, cored, and cut into ½-inch pieces
12 ounces fresh cranberries
½ cup unsweetened apple juice

1½ teaspoons kosher salt
½ teaspoon freshly ground black pepper
8 turkey cutlets, each 3 to 4 ounces and about ½ inch thick

½ cup granulated sugar
¼ teaspoon ground cloves
¼ teaspoon kosher salt

1. In a shallow baking dish, combine the oil, sage, garlic, salt, and pepper and mix well. Put the cutlets in the dish and turn to coat them evenly. Set aside at room temperature for up to 20 minutes while you make the sauce. 2. In a medium saucepan over medium-high heat, combine all the sauce ingredients and bring to a boil on the stove. Turn down the heat to a simmer, cover, and cook until all the cranberries have popped, 6 to 10 minutes. Set aside to cool. 3. Set Traeger temperature to 400°F and preheat, lid closed for 15 minutes. 4. Grill the cutlets, with the lid closed, until the meat is firm to the touch and no longer pink in the center, 4 to 6 minutes, turning once. Remove the cutlets from the grill and serve warm with the sauce spooned on top.

Honey-Lemon Glazed Chicken Thighs

Prep Time: 20 minutes | Cook Time: 40 minutes | Serves: 4

Glaze:
2 teaspoons extra-virgin olive oil
3 medium garlic cloves, minced or pushed through a press
1 tablespoon peeled, grated fresh ginger
½ cup honey
Rub:
1 teaspoon dried marjoram
1 teaspoon dried basil
1 teaspoon garlic powder
1 teaspoon kosher salt

3 tablespoons fresh lemon juice
2 teaspoons cornstarch dissolved in 2 teaspoons water
1 teaspoon finely grated lemon zest

¾ teaspoon freshly ground black pepper
¼ teaspoon ground cinnamon
8 chicken thighs (with bone and skin), each 5–6 ounces, trimmed of excess fat and skin

1. Set Traeger temperature to 400°F and preheat, lid closed for 15 minutes. 2. In a small saucepan over medium-high heat, warm the oil. Stir in the garlic and the ginger and cook until they just start to brown, 1 to 2 minutes, stirring often. Add the honey, bring to a boil, and cook for 2 minutes, watching carefully and reducing the heat if necessary so the mixture doesn't boil over. Add the lemon juice and cook for 1 minute. Stir in the cornstarch mixture, return to a boil, and cook until slightly thickened, about 1 minute. Remove from the heat and stir in the lemon zest. The glaze will continue to thicken as it cools. 3. Combine the rub ingredients. Season the chicken thighs evenly with the rub. 4. Grill the chicken, skin side down first, with the lid closed, until golden brown, 6 to 10 minutes, turning occasionally. Brush with some of the glaze, and cook until the juices run clear and the meat is no longer pink at the bone, about 30 minutes more, turning once or twice and occasionally brushing with the remaining glaze. Remove from the grill and let rest for 3 to 5 minutes. Serve warm.

Grilled Chicken Drumsticks and Peaches

Prep Time: 20 minutes | Cook Time: 30 minutes | Serves: 4

Glaze:

1 cup peach preserves
½ cup peach nectar
4 teaspoons prepared chili powder
1 teaspoon finely grated lime zest
2 tablespoons fresh lime juice
½ cup chopped fresh cilantro leaves

Kosher salt
Freshly ground black pepper
12 chicken drumsticks, 2 ¾–3 pounds total
4 firm but ripe peaches, each cut in half
2 teaspoons canola oil

1. In a small saucepan over medium-high heat, combine the preserves, nectar, and chili powder. Bring to a simmer, whisking until the mixture is well blended and almost smooth, about 1 minute. Remove the saucepan from the heat and whisk in the lime zest and juice. Let cool to lukewarm, then whisk in the cilantro, V teaspoon salt, and V teaspoon pepper. 2. Divide the glaze equally between two small bowls: one for brushing on the chicken while grilling and the other for serving. 3. Set Traeger temperature to 400°F and preheat, lid closed for 15 minutes. 4. Pat the drumsticks dry with paper towels and season evenly with 1¼ teaspoons salt and 1 teaspoon pepper. Brush the cut side of the peach halves lightly with the oil. 5. Grill the drumsticks, with the lid closed, until the skin is golden brown and the meat is almost firm to the touch, about 20 minutes, turning occasionally. Brush the peach glaze from the first bowl evenly over the drumsticks. Continue grilling, with the lid closed, until the juices run clear and the meat is no longer pink at the bone, 5 to 10 minutes more, turning once or twice and brushing occasionally with more of the glaze. 6. During the last 5 minutes of grilling time, grill the peach halves, cut side down, until lightly charred and beginning to soften (check after 3 minutes). Remove the drumsticks and the peaches from the grill and let the drumsticks rest for 3 to 5 minutes. Serve the drumsticks and the peaches warm with the reserved glaze.

Spiced Chicken with Orange-Chipotle Barbecue Sauce

Prep Time: 30 minutes | Cook Time: 40 minutes | Serves: 4

Rub:

1½ teaspoons kosher salt
1 teaspoon freshly ground black pepper
1 teaspoon granulated garlic
1 teaspoon dried thyme

Sauce:

½ cup minced yellow onion
2 garlic cloves, minced or pushed through a press
1 cup fresh orange juice
1 cup ketchup
2 canned chipotle chile peppers in adobo sauce, minced

¼ teaspoon ground allspice
4 whole chicken legs, each 10–12 ounces, excess skin and fat removed
Extra-virgin olive oil

1 tablespoon packed golden brown sugar
1 tablespoon cider vinegar
1 teaspoon Worcestershire sauce
¼ teaspoon ground allspice

1. Set Traeger temperature to 400°F and preheat, lid closed for 15 minutes. 2. Combine the rub ingredients. Lightly brush the chicken on both sides with oil and season evenly with the rub. 3. In a small saucepan over medium heat, warm 2 tablespoons oil. Add the onion and the garlic and cook until the onion is tender but not browned, 3 to 5 minutes, stirring occasionally. Add the remaining sauce ingredients and whisk until smooth. Simmer over medium heat for 5 to 7 minutes, stirring occasionally. Remove from the heat. 4. Grill the chicken, skin side up, with the lid closed, until the juices run clear and the meat is no longer pink at the bone, 35 to 40 minutes, brushing once with the sauce after 30 minutes. Brush with the sauce again and continue cooking, with the lid open, until the skin is well browned, 5 to 10 minutes more, turning once or twice. Remove from the grill and let rest for 3 to 5 minutes. 5. Serve the chicken warm with the remaining sauce.

Teriyaki Chicken Skewers

Prep Time: 15 minutes | Cook Time: 10 minutes | Serves: 8

6 to 8 boneless, skinless chicken thighs, cut into 1-inch cubes
Salt
Freshly ground black pepper
Avocado oil spray

1 cup Sticky Honey Teriyaki Sauce, divided
1 tablespoon toasted sesame seeds
2 to 3 scallions, sliced

1. Skewer the cubed chicken thighs onto six to eight wood or metal skewers. Season them lightly with salt and pepper and set aside. 2. Set Traeger temperature to 450°F and preheat, lid closed for 15 minutes. 3. Spray the chicken skewers with avocado oil. 4. When the grill is up to temperature, place the chicken skewers on the grill grate. Close the lid and cook for 1 to 2 minutes. Open the lid and give the skewers a quarter turn, close the lid, and cook for another 1 to 2 minutes. Open the lid, give the skewers another quarter turn, and cook for 1 to 2 minutes more. After 1 to 2 minutes, open the lid and test the internal temperature of the thighs. When the chicken reaches 162°F to 163°F, brush it with ¼ cup of teriyaki sauce. Cook for 2 to 3 minutes, flip the skewers, brush them again with ¼ cup of teriyaki sauce, and cook for 2 to 3 minutes more. At this point, test the internal temperature to make sure it is at least 165°F before removing the thighs from the grill. 5. Place the cooked thighs on a plate and let rest for 5 to 10 minutes, loosely covered with aluminum foil. When ready to serve, place the skewers on a serving plate and top with toasted sesame seeds and sliced scallions. Serve with the remaining teriyaki sauce on the side.

Chapter 4 Beef Recipes

50 Garlicky Prime Rib Roast

50 Bacon and Mushroom Beef Burgers

50 Grilled Flank Steak with Chimichurri

51 Spiced Rib Eyes Steaks

51 BBQ Beef Brisket

51 Chimichurri Beef

52 Classic Beef Hamburgers

52 Garlic-Thyme Prime Rib Roast

52 Beef-Bacon Cheeseburgers

53 Steak-Mushroom Kebabs with Yum Yum Sauce

53 Sweet & Spicy Tri-Tip Roast with Corn-Bean Salad

54 Spicy Beef Kabobs with Pineapple Salsa

54 Skirt Steak Skewers with Green Chile Sauce

55 Sweet and Sour Short Ribs

55 Roast Beef, Potato and Egg Skillet

56 Garlic T-Bone Steak with Blue Cheese Butter

56 Herbed Tri-Tip Sirloin

56 Grilled Meat Loaf

57 Delicious Barbecue Beef Back Ribs

57 Garlic Prime Rib

57 Rosemary Veal Chops with Red Pepper-Butter Sauce

58 Barbecue Pulled Beef

58 Flavorful Pepper Steak Stir-Fry

58 Thyme Flank Steak with Balsamic Pearl Onions

59 Korean-Inspired Short Ribs

59 Garlic Beef Tenderloin with Romesco Sauce

59 California French Beef Roast

60 Garlic New York Strip Roast

60 Horseradish-Crusted Rib Roast with Butter Gravy

60 Caramelizd Beef Slices

61 Grilled Hot Dogs with Spicy Pickled Vegetables

61 Parmesan Meatballs

61 Grilled T-Bone Steaks with Moroccan Spice Paste

Garlicky Prime Rib Roast

Prep Time: 20 minutes | Cook Time: 4 hours | Serves: 10

1 (6-pound) prime rib roast
1 tablespoon olive oil
8 garlic cloves, minced
1 tablespoon finely minced shallots
2 tablespoons butter, softened

2½ tablespoons Dijon mustard
2 tablespoons coarse salt
1 tablespoon finely chopped fresh rosemary
1 tablespoon finely chopped fresh marjoram
1 tablespoon coarsely ground black pepper

1. Trim any loose pieces of fat or meat from the roast. 2. Heat the olive oil in a small skillet over low heat. Add the garlic and shallots. Sauté for 2 minutes or until slightly translucent, then remove from heat. 3. In a medium bowl, combine the softened butter, Dijon mustard, salt, rosemary, marjoram, and black pepper to make a paste. Add the garlic and shallots and stir to combine. 4. Coat the roast evenly with the seasoning rub. 5. Set Traeger temperature to 250°F and preheat, lid closed for 15 minutes. Place the roast on the grill grate and close the lid. Cook for 2 hours. 6. After 2 hours, flip the roast for even cooking and continue cooking for another 2 hours, or until the prime rib reaches an internal temperature of 120°F to 125°F (medium-rare). Remove, tent with foil, and let rest for 20 to 30 minutes before carving.

Bacon and Mushroom Beef Burgers

Prep Time: 10 minutes | Cook Time: 20 minutes | Serves: 4

8 bacon slices
8 ounces cremini mushrooms, sliced
Kosher salt
Freshly ground black pepper

2 pounds ground beef
4 Swiss cheese slices
4 kaiser rolls, split
½ cup aioli

1. Set Traeger temperature to 500°F and preheat, lid closed for 15 minutes. Then preheat a 10-inch cast iron skillet on the grate with the lid closed. 2. Put the bacon in the skillet. Close the lid and cook for 1 to 2 minutes or until browned and crispy around the edges. Transfer to a plate. 3. Add the mushrooms to the skillet. Close the lid and cook, stirring once, for 7 to 9 minutes or until browned. Transfer to a plate. Season with salt and pepper. 4. Meanwhile, in a large bowl, season the beef with pepper and 4 teaspoons of salt. Using your hands, mix until just incorporated; form into four 1-inch-thick patties with a slight dimple in the center. 5. Put the burgers on the grill grate. Close the lid and cook, flipping halfway through, for 8 to 10 minutes total for medium, or until an instant-read thermometer inserted into the center registers 135°F. (If using store-bought ground beef, always cook it to 160°F, or well done.) In the last minute of cooking, top the patties with the cheese to melt and place the rolls cut-side down on the grate to toast. 6. Spread the aioli on the buns and assemble the burgers, dividing the bacon and mushrooms between them. Serve immediately.

Grilled Flank Steak with Chimichurri

Prep Time: 5 minutes | Cook Time: 6 minutes | Serves: 8

1 (2½-pound) flank steak
Kosher salt
Vegetable oil, for coating the steak

Freshly ground black pepper
½ cup chimichurri

1. Season the steak generously with salt on both sides. Refrigerate overnight. 2. Pat the steak dry. 3. Set Traeger temperature to 650°F and preheat, lid closed for 15 minutes. 4. Lightly coat the steak with oil. 5. Put on the grill grate. Close the lid and cook, flipping halfway through, for 6 minutes total for medium, or until an instant-read thermometer inserted into the thickest part registers 135°F. 6. Remove from the heat. Season with pepper. Rest for 10 minutes before slicing thinly across the grain at a 45-degree angle. Serve with the chimichurri on the side.

Spiced Rib Eyes Steaks

Prep Time: 20 minutes | Cook Time: 2 hours | Serves: 4

3 tablespoons flaked sea salt
3 tablespoons dark brown sugar
2 tablespoons sweet paprika
1 tablespoon garlic powder
1 tablespoon dried mustard

1 tablespoon freshly ground black pepper
1 tablespoon dried oregano
1 teaspoon ground coriander
1 teaspoon ground cumin
2 (2-inch thick) bone-in tomahawk rib eye steaks

1. In a large bowl, whisk together the salt, sugar, paprika, garlic powder, mustard, pepper, oregano, coriander, and cumin. Season the steaks on all sides with the dry rub. Cover the steaks with plastic wrap and refrigerate them for 24 hours. 2. Remove the steaks from the refrigerator 20 minutes before cooking. 3. Set Traeger temperature to 275°F and preheat, lid closed for 15 minutes. 4. Place the steaks on the grill grate, leaving space between them. Insert a probe thermometer (if available) into the thickest part of the meat, not touching the bone. Set the target temperature for 125°F for rare, 135°F for medium-rare, 145°F for medium, 150°F for medium-well, and 160°F for well-done. Smoke for about 2 hours, or until the internal thermometer reads 5°F lower than your desired doneness. 5. Transfer the steaks to a cutting board, loosely tent them with aluminum foil, and let them rest for 15 minutes. The temperature of the beef will continue to rise while resting, achieving desired doneness. 6. Serve as desired.

BBQ Beef Brisket

Prep Time: 30 minutes | Cook Time: 8 hours | Serves: 8

3 tablespoons dark brown sugar
2 tablespoons chili powder
2 tablespoons smoked paprika
2 tablespoons fine sea salt
1 tablespoon ground cumin

1 tablespoon dried mustard
1 teaspoon ground cayenne pepper
7 pounds beef brisket (flat cut), trimmed and excess fat removed
Flaked sea salt
Freshly ground black pepper

1. In a large bowl, whisk together the sugar, chili powder, paprika, salt, cumin, mustard, and cayenne. Season the brisket on all sides with this dry rub and wrap it tightly in plastic wrap. Refrigerate it for 24 hours. 2. Remove the brisket from the refrigerator 20 minutes before cooking. Remove the plastic wrap. Season the meat all over with salt and pepper. 3. Set Traeger temperature to 200°F and preheat, lid closed for 15 minutes. 4. Place the brisket on the grill grate and cook for 5 hours. 5. Remove the brisket from the grill and wrap it in aluminum foil. Place the wrapped brisket on a baking sheet and return it to the grill. Insert a probe thermometer (if available) into the thickest part of the meat. Set the target temperature for 190°F. Cook the brisket for about 3 hours more, or until the target internal temperature is reached. 6. Transfer the brisket to a cutting board. Remove the foil and loosely tent the meat with it. Let the meat rest for 30 minutes before slicing and serving it.

Chimichurri Beef

Prep Time: 20 minutes | Cook Time: 1 hour | Serves: 4

1 bunch fresh flat-leaf parsley, leaves stripped and chopped
1 garlic bulb, cloves separated, peeled, and crushed
1 cup extra-virgin olive oil
Grated zest of 1 lemon, plus 1 lemon, halved, for serving

Grated zest of 1 lime, plus juice of 1 lime
Flaked sea salt
Freshly ground black pepper
4 (2-inch-thick) beef striploins, trimmed and excess fat removed

1. In a large bowl, whisk together the parsley, garlic, olive oil, lemon zest, and lime zest. Add the lime juice and season with salt and pepper. Refrigerate until needed. 2. Set Traeger temperature to 275°F and preheat, lid closed for 15 minutes. 3. If refrigerated, allow the steaks to rest at room temperature for 15-20 minutes before cooking. Season the striploin on both sides with salt and pepper. Rub half the chimichurri sauce over the steaks. Insert a probe thermometer (if available) into the thickest part of the meat. Set the target temperature for 125°F for rare, 135°F for medium-rare, 145°F for medium, 150°F for medium-well, and 160°F for well-done. Place the meat on the grill grate and cook for about 1 hour. Remove the steaks from the grill when the thermometer reads 5°F lower than your desired doneness. 4. Transfer the steaks to a cutting board, loosely tent them with aluminum foil, and let them rest for 10 minutes. The temperature of the beef will continue to rise while resting, achieving desired doneness. 5. Taste and season with salt and pepper, as needed. Thinly slice the steak across the grain and serve with the remaining half of the chimichurri sauce and a squeeze of fresh lemon juice.

Classic Beef Hamburgers

Prep Time: 10 minutes | Cook Time: 7 minutes | Serves: 4

1 pound 80% or 85% lean ground beef
1 teaspoon salt

1 teaspoon black pepper
4 burger buns

1. Divide the ground meat into 4 portions. Gently flatten each portion into a round, flat circle about ½ inch thick. Generously season the burgers with salt and pepper. 2. Set Traeger temperature to 450°F and preheat, lid closed for 15 minutes. 3. Oil the grill grates, then place the beef patties on the grill grate, uncovered, for 3 to 4 minutes on each side, until the internal temperature reaches 160°F. 4. Place the buns, cut-side down, on the grill grate and cook for 1 to 2 minutes to toast. Put the burgers on the toasted buns and add your favorite toppings. Eat immediately—if not sooner!

Garlic-Thyme Prime Rib Roast

Prep Time: 20 minutes | Cook Time: 3 hours | Serves: 4

4 pounds bone-in (2 guests per bone) prime rib roast, trimmed and excess fat removed
1 garlic bulb, cloves separated, peeled, and halved
4 thyme sprigs, leaves stripped
2 tablespoons Italian seasoning
1 tablespoon ground paprika

1 tablespoon onion powder
1 tablespoon ground coriander
1 tablespoon coarsely ground black pepper
3 tablespoons extra-virgin olive oil, for drizzling
Coarse sea salt
Freshly ground black pepper

1. Remove the roast from the refrigerator 1 hour before preparation. 2. Set Traeger temperature to 275°F and preheat, lid closed for 15 minutes. 3. Using a boning knife, make incisions into the roast deep enough to press in half of a garlic clove below the surface of the meat. Space the incisions evenly so each slice of beef will have several cloves in it. Insert ½ garlic clove into each incision. 4. In a medium bowl, whisk together the thyme, Italian seasoning, paprika, onion powder, coriander, and pepper. 5. Drizzle the roast with the olive oil and massage the spice mixture all over the roast. Season with salt and pepper. Insert a probe thermometer (if available) into the thickest part of the meat, not touching the bone. Set the target temperature for 125°F for rare, 135°F for medium-rare, 145°F for medium, 150°F for medium-well, and 160°F for well-done. Place the roast, fat-side up (rib bones down), on the grill grate. Cook for 3 to 4 hours. 6. Remove the roast from the grill when the thermometer reads 5°F lower than your desired doneness. The temperature of the beef will continue to rise while resting, achieving desired doneness. 7. Transfer the roast to a cutting board, loosely tent it with aluminum foil, and let it rest for 30 minutes before slicing and serving it.

Beef-Bacon Cheeseburgers

Prep Time: 10 minutes | Cook Time: 10 minutes | Serves: 4

1½ pounds ground beef
6 slices cooked and crumbled bacon
1 (8-ounce) block cheddar cheese
1 tablespoon Worcestershire sauce

Kosher salt and freshly ground black pepper
4 burger buns
Toppings of choice, such as ketchup, lettuce, pickles, etc.

1. In a large bowl, combine the ground beef and bacon. 2. Cut the block of cheese in half. Cut one half into tiny cubes and add those cubes to the bowl with the ground beef and bacon. Cut the other half of the block of cheese into four thin slices and set aside. 3. Add the Worcestershire sauce, salt, and pepper to the ground beef. Mix with your hands until evenly combined, then form into four burger patties. 4. Set Traeger temperature to 500°F and preheat, lid closed for 15 minutes. 5. Once preheated, put the burgers on the grill grate. Grill for 8 to 10 minutes, flip them halfway through the cooking time. Top burgers with the sliced cheddar cheese during the last minute or two of cooking. 6. Serve on burger buns with toppings of choice.

Steak-Mushroom Kebabs with Yum Yum Sauce

Prep Time: 15 minutes | Cook Time: 15 minutes | Serves: 4

⅔ cup mayonnaise
¼ cup ketchup
1 tablespoon sugar
1 teaspoon paprika
1 teaspoon garlic powder
3 tablespoons soy sauce
1 tablespoon honey
1½ tablespoons ginger paste

1½ tablespoons garlic paste
1½ pounds flat iron steak
8 to 10 kebab skewers (if using wooden skewers, soak in water for at least 30 minutes before placing on the grill to prevent burning)
8 ounces baby portobello mushrooms, roughly cut into bite-size chunks
1 onion, roughly cut into bite-size chunks

1. In a bowl, combine the mayonnaise, ketchup, sugar, paprika, and garlic powder. Whisk until evenly combined. Store this yum sauce in a covered container in the refrigerator until ready to use. 2. In another bowl, whisk together the soy sauce, honey, ginger paste, and garlic paste until evenly combined. 3. Cut the steak into bite-size cubes and place the cubes in a gallon-size plastic bag. Add half of the soy sauce mixture to the steak. Massage the bag until the steak is evenly coated. Marinate in the refrigerator for several hours or overnight. Store the remaining soy sauce mixture in the refrigerator. 4. When ready to cook, set Traeger temperature to 450°F and preheat, lid closed for 15 minutes.

Toss the mushroom and onion chunks with the remaining soy sauce mixture. 5. Thread the steak, mushrooms, and onions onto skewers. Place the skewers on the grill grate and cook for 15 to 18 minutes, turning halfway through. 6. Serve the kebabs immediately with the yum sauce on the side.

Sweet & Spicy Tri-Tip Roast with Corn-Bean Salad

Prep Time: 20 minutes | Cook Time: 30 minutes | Serves: 8

3 ears fresh corn, husked
Extra-virgin olive oil
3 tablespoons fresh lime juice
1 garlic clove, minced or pushed through a press
1 teaspoon dried oregano
Kosher salt
Rub:
1 tablespoon coarsely ground espresso
2 teaspoons prepared chili powder
2 teaspoons packed golden brown sugar
1 teaspoon dried oregano

Freshly ground black pepper
1 can (15 ounces) pinto beans, rinsed and drained
2 scallions, ends trimmed and finely chopped
½ medium red bell pepper, cut into ½-inch dice
1 jalapeño chile pepper, seeded and minced

¼ teaspoon granulated garlic
¼ teaspoon granulated onion
1 tri-tip roast, about 2 ¾ pounds and 2 inches thick, trimmed of silver skin and any excess fat

1. Set Traeger temperature to 400°F and preheat, lid closed for 15 minutes. 2. Brush the corn with oil and place on the grill grate, with the lid closed, grill until browned in spots and tender, 8 to 10 minutes, turning occasionally. Remove from the grill, and let cool.

In a large bowl, whisk the lime juice, garlic, oregano, ½ teaspoon salt, and ½ teaspoon pepper. Slowly whisk in ⅓ cup oil. Add the pinto beans, scallions, bell pepper, and jalapeño. Cut off the corn kernels and add them to the salad. 3. Combine the rub ingredients, including 1 teaspoon salt and ½ teaspoon pepper. Brush the roast on both sides with oil and season evenly with the rub. Allow the roast to stand at room temperature for 15 to 30 minutes. 4. Grill the roast, with the lid closed, until well marked on both sides, 30 to 35 minutes, turning every 5 minutes. Remove from the grill and let rest for 5 to 10 minutes. Cut the roast across the grain into thin slices and serve with the salad.

Spicy Beef Kabobs with Pineapple Salsa

Prep Time: 20 minutes | Cook Time: 8 minutes | Serves: 4

Marinade:

1 Scotch bonnet or habanero chile pepper
3 scallions (white and green parts only), chopped
⅓ cup roughly chopped fresh basil leaves
¼ cup canola oil
2 tablespoons cider vinegar
2 tablespoons packed dark brown sugar

1 tablespoon minced fresh ginger
1 teaspoon minced garlic
1 teaspoon ground allspice
1 teaspoon kosher salt
2 pounds top sirloin, about 1 ¼ inches thick, trimmed of excess fat, cut into 1 ¼-inch cubes

Salsa:

½ medium pineapple, cut into ¼-inch cubes
1 medium red bell pepper, finely chopped
1 scallion (white and light green parts only), finely chopped

2 tablespoons finely chopped fresh basil leaves
1 teaspoon cider vinegar
¼ teaspoon kosher salt

1. If using bamboo skewers, soak in water for at least 30 minutes. 2. Wearing rubber gloves (to avoid burning your skin), remove and discard the stem and seeds from the chile. Put the chile in a food processor along with the remaining marinade ingredients, and process until smooth. 3. Place the meat cubes in a large, resealable plastic bag and pour in the marinade. Press the air out of the bag and seal tightly. Turn the bag to distribute the marinade, place in a bowl, and refrigerate for 2 to 4 hours. 4. Wearing rubber gloves, thread the meat onto skewers and allow to stand at room temperature for 15 to 30 minutes before grilling. Discard the marinade. 5. Set Traeger temperature to 500°F and preheat, lid closed for 15 minutes. 6. Combine the salsa ingredients. 7. Grill the kabobs, with the lid closed, until the meat is cooked to your desired doneness, 6 to 8 minutes for medium rare, turning occasionally. Remove the kabobs from the grill and serve warm with the salsa.

Skirt Steak Skewers with Green Chile Sauce

Prep Time: 40 minutes | Cook Time: 15 minutes | Serves: 4

Marinade:

½ cup dark beer
2 tablespoons fresh lime juice
2 tablespoons packed dark brown sugar
1 tablespoon hot chili-garlic sauce, such as Sriracha
1 tablespoon Dijon mustard
1 tablespoon vegetable oil

2 teaspoons ground cumin
2 garlic cloves, minced or pushed through a press
1 teaspoon paprika
1 teaspoon kosher salt
1½ pounds skirt steak, about ½ inch thick, trimmed of excess surface fat

Sauce:

1 large green bell pepper
2 garlic cloves
1 cup loosely packed fresh cilantro leaves and tender stems
1 jalapeño chile pepper, seeded and roughly chopped
½ medium poblano or pasilla chile pepper, seeded and roughly chopped

2 tablespoons extra-virgin olive oil
1 tablespoon fresh lime juice
1 teaspoon kosher salt
½ teaspoon ground cumin
½ teaspoon freshly ground black pepper

1. Whisk the marinade ingredients. 2. Cut the steak crosswise into four equal pieces. Then cut each piece lengthwise in half (against the grain). Place the steak pieces in a large, resealable plastic bag and pour in the marinade. Press the air out of the bag and seal tightly. Turn the bag to distribute the marinade, place in a bowl, and refrigerate for 4 to 6 hours, turning occasionally. 3. If using bamboo skewers, soak in water for at least 30 minutes. 4. Set Traeger temperature to 400°F and preheat, lid closed for 15 minutes. 5. Grill the bell pepper with the lid closed, until blackened and blistered all over, 10 to 12 minutes, turning occasionally. Put the pepper in a bowl and cover with plastic wrap to trap the steam. Let stand for about 10 minutes. Remove the pepper from the bowl and peel away and discard the charred skin. Cut off and discard the stem and seeds, and then roughly chop the pepper. Place the pepper and the garlic in a food processor and pulse until finely chopped. Add the remaining sauce ingredients and process to a chunky paste. Transfer to a bowl. Stir the sauce just before serving. 6. Increase the temperature of the grill to 500°F. 7. Remove the steak from the bag and discard the marinade. Thread the steak pieces onto skewers. 8. Grill the skewers with the lid closed, until cooked to your desired doneness, 4 to 6 minutes for medium rare, turning once. Remove from the grill and serve warm with the sauce.

Sweet and Sour Short Ribs

Prep Time: 25 minutes | Cook Time: 2-3 hours | Serves: 6

Braising Liquid:

1 tablespoon extra-virgin olive oil
1 large yellow onion, chopped
4 garlic cloves, chopped
1 can (14 ½ ounces) diced fire-roasted tomatoes in juice
1 cup merlot
1 cup low-sodium beef broth

1 tablespoon Italian herb seasoning
1 teaspoon kosher salt
½ teaspoon freshly ground black pepper
12 meaty bone-in beef short ribs, about 7 ½ pounds total, each 3–4 inches long

Glaze:

⅓ cup balsamic vinegar
¼ cup packed golden brown sugar

3 tablespoons tomato paste

1. Set Traeger temperature to 350°F and preheat, lid closed for 15 minutes. 2. In a medium saucepan over medium-high heat, warm the oil. Add the onion and cook until softened, about 3 minutes, stirring occasionally. Stir in the garlic and cook until fragrant, about 1 minute. Add the remaining braising liquid ingredients and bring to a boil. Arrange the ribs, bone side down, in a single layer in a large disposable foil pan. Pour the braising liquid over the ribs and cover the pan tightly with aluminum foil. Place the pan directly on the grill grate. Close the lid and cook until the ribs are very tender when pierced with the tip of a knife, 1½ to 2 hours. Transfer the ribs to a platter and tent loosely with foil. 3. Allow the braising liquid in the pan to stand for 5 minutes, then skim the fat from the surface. Pour half of the liquid into a blender, add the glaze ingredients, and puree until smooth. Transfer to a bowl. Pour the remaining liquid in the blender, puree, and add to the bowl. Pour the glaze back into the foil pan and cook, with the lid closed, until thickened and reduced, about 25 minutes, stirring frequently. 4. Return the ribs to the grill, close the lid, brush with some of the glaze, and cook until warmed through and nicely marked, 10 to 15 minutes, turning often and brushing with more glaze at each turn. Serve the ribs warm with any remaining glaze.

Roast Beef, Potato and Egg Skillet

Prep Time: 20 minutes | Cook Time: 2 hours | Serves: 4

2 pounds eye of round roast, trimmed
2 tablespoons extra-virgin olive oil
2 tablespoons unsalted butter
Paprika, for seasoning
Flaked sea salt
Freshly ground black pepper
8 new red potatoes, blanched and diced

1 yellow onion, diced
1 red bell pepper, cored and diced
4 garlic cloves, minced
4 thyme sprigs, leaves stripped, plus more for garnish
2 ears corn, kernels cut off
4 flat-leaf parsley sprigs, leaves stripped and finely chopped
8 large eggs

1. Remove the roast from the refrigerator 20 minutes before preparation. 2. Set Traeger temperature to 250°F and preheat, lid closed for 15 minutes. 3. Place a large cast iron skillet the grill to preheat, then pour in the olive oil and add the butter to melt. 4. Season the roast all over with paprika, salt, and pepper. Place the roast on the grill grate. Insert a probe thermometer (if available) into the thickest part of the meat, not touching the bone. Set the target temperature for 125°F for rare, 135°F for medium-rare, 145°F for medium, 150°F for medium-well, and 160°F for well-done. Cook the meat for 30 minutes. 5. In the skillet, combine the potatoes, onion, red bell pepper, garlic, and thyme. Season with salt and pepper. Cook for about 90 minutes more, or until the internal thermometer reads 5°F lower than desired doneness. Remove the skillet and the roast from the grill. The temperature of the beef will continue to rise while resting, achieving desired doneness. 6. Transfer the roast to a cutting board, loosely tent it with aluminum foil, and let it rest for 20 minutes. Thinly slice the beef and add it to the skillet, along with the corn and parsley. Toss to incorporate. Place the skillet back on the grill and cook for 10 minutes. 7. Crack the eggs into the hash, leaving space between them for individual portions. Season with salt and pepper. Cook the eggs to your desired doneness. Serve garnished with thyme.

Garlic T-Bone Steak with Blue Cheese Butter

Prep Time: 10 minutes | Cook Time: 45 minutes | Serves: 4

4 tablespoons (½ stick) unsalted butter, at room temperature
½ cup blue cheese crumbles
4 (14-ounce, 1-inch-thick) T-bone steaks

2 tablespoons kosher salt
1 tablespoon freshly ground black pepper
2 tablespoons minced garlic

1. In a medium bowl, stir together the butter and blue cheese crumbles and set aside, but do not refrigerate unless making in advance. 2. Set Traeger temperature to 165°F and preheat, lid closed for 15 minutes. 3. Season the steaks with the salt, pepper, and garlic. 4. Arrange the steaks directly on the grill, close the lid, and grill for 30 minutes. 5. Increase the heat to 450°F and grill for an additional 15 minutes for medium-rare, or longer for desired doneness, turning once, until a meat thermometer inserted in the meat reads 120°F to 155°F. 6. Remove the steaks from the grill and let rest for 3 to 5 minutes before serving topped with the blue cheese butter.

Herbed Tri-Tip Sirloin

Prep Time: 15 minutes | Cook Time: 45 minutes | Serves: 6

2 teaspoons sea salt
2 teaspoons freshly ground black pepper
2 teaspoons onion powder
2 teaspoons garlic powder
2 teaspoons dried oregano

1 teaspoon cayenne pepper
1 teaspoon ground sage
1 teaspoon finely chopped fresh rosemary
1 (1½ – to 2-pound) tri-tip bottom sirloin

1. Set Traeger temperature to 425°F and preheat, lid closed for 15 minutes. 2. In a small bowl, combine the salt, pepper, onion powder, garlic powder, oregano, cayenne pepper, sage, and rosemary to create a rub. 3. Season the meat all over with the rub and lay it directly on the grill grate. 4. Close the lid and smoke for 45 minutes to 1 hour, or until a meat thermometer inserted in the thickest part of the meat reads 120°F for rare, 130°F for medium-rare, or 140°F for medium, keeping in mind that the meat will come up in temperature by about another 5°F during the rest period. 5. Remove the tri-tip from the heat, tent with aluminum foil, and let rest for 15 minutes before slicing against the grain.

Grilled Meat Loaf

Prep Time: 15 minutes | Cook Time: 2 hours | Serves: 8

1½ cups seasoned (your choice of flavor) bread crumbs
3 tablespoons finely chopped onion
2 cloves garlic, minced
½ teaspoon kosher salt
½ teaspoon dried oregano
½ teaspoon dried thyme

½ teaspoon crushed dried rosemary
¼ teaspoon freshly ground black pepper
½ cup half-and-half
1 pound each ground beef, veal, and pork (or any combination you prefer)
Your favorite marinara sauce for serving

1. In a large bowl, combine the bread crumbs, onion, garlic, salt, oregano, thyme, rosemary, and pepper and stir well to combine. Pour in the half-and-half and stir to combine. Add the meat and, using your hands, mix until thoroughly combined. 2. Spray a 9- × 13-inch disposable aluminum-foil pan with cooking spray. Place the meat mixture in the pan and form into a loaf around 3 inches wide and 8 inches long. 3. Set Traeger temperature to 200°F and preheat, lid closed for 15 minutes. 4. Put the pan on the grill, close the lid, and smoke for about 2 hours, until the internal temperature in the center reaches 150° to 160° F. The meat loaf is going to take on a pretty pinkish-brown hue as it smokes. 5. When done, remove from the grill and, using two spatulas, lift the meat loaf from the pan onto a platter. Tent with aluminum foil and let rest a good 30 minutes. Slice and serve with warm marinara sauce.

Delicious Barbecue Beef Back Ribs

Prep Time: 15 minutes | Cook Time: 4 hours | Serves: 4

2 racks (6 to 8 bones each or equivalent) beef back ribs
2 tablespoons salt

1 tablespoon black pepper
1 cup Kansas City–Style Barbecue Sauce

1. Generously season the beef ribs with salt and pepper, covering the surface well. 2. Set Traeger temperature to 300°F and preheat, lid closed for 15 minutes. 3. Place the ribs on the grill. Close the lid and cook for 4 to 5 hours, turning once every hour. The ribs are fully cooked when the meat pulls back from the bones and the meat feels tender (with no resistance) when probed with a metal skewer or meat thermometer. 4. Brush the ribs with barbecue sauce during the last 5 to 10 minutes of cook time, turning every 2 to 3 minutes. 5. Let the ribs rest for 10 to 15 minutes, then cut into individual portions and serve immediately with any remaining barbecue sauce on the side.

Garlic Prime Rib

Prep Time: 10 minutes | Cook Time: 2 hours | Serves: 6

¼ cup olive oil
4 garlic cloves, minced
3 teaspoons salt
1 teaspoon paprika

1 teaspoon ground fresh rosemary leaves
¾ teaspoon black pepper
1 (4- to 5-pound) boneless beef rib roast

1. In a small bowl, stir together the olive oil, garlic, salt, paprika, rosemary, and pepper to blend. Spread the seasoning mixture evenly over all surfaces of the beef. Put the beef on a plate, cover, and let sit at room temperature for 1 hour. 2. Set Traeger temperature to 300°F and preheat, lid closed for 15 minutes. 3. Place the beef on the grill grate. Close the lid and cook for about 2 hours, or until the internal temperature of the beef reaches 110°F for rare or 115°F for medium-rare (the beef will continue to cook as it rests, up to 10 or 15 degrees more). 4. Transfer the beef to a plate and loosely cover the beef with aluminum foil and let rest for 15 minutes. Cut the beef into ½-inch-thick slices, or as desired. Serve immediately.

Rosemary Veal Chops with Red Pepper-Butter Sauce

Prep Time: 20 minutes | Cook Time: 8 minutes | Serves: 4

2 tablespoons extra-virgin olive oil
2 teaspoons finely chopped fresh rosemary leaves
1 teaspoon minced garlic
Sauce:
¼ cup (½ stick) unsalted butter
¾ teaspoon finely chopped fresh rosemary leaves
2 small red bell peppers, thinly sliced

¾ teaspoon kosher salt
¼ teaspoon freshly ground black pepper
4 veal rib chops, each about 12 ounces and 1 inch thick

2 tablespoons capers, drained
1½ tablespoons fresh lemon juice
¼ teaspoon kosher salt

1. Combine the oil, rosemary, garlic, salt, and pepper. Brush the veal chops on both sides with the oil mixture. Allow the chops to stand at room temperature for 15 to 30 minutes before grilling. 2. Set Traeger temperature to 500°F and preheat, lid closed for 15 minutes. 3. Place the chops on the grill grate, with the lid closed, until cooked to your desired doneness, 6 to 8 minutes for medium rare, turning once. Remove from the grill and let rest while you make the sauce. 4. In a small skillet over medium-high heat, melt the butter and then add the rosemary. Cook until the milk solids are toasted and the butter has a nutty smell, 2 to 4 minutes, stirring occasionally. Add the bell peppers and cook until slightly softened, about 2 minutes, stirring once or twice. Add the capers and lemon juice and cook for 1 minute. Remove the skillet from the heat and stir in the salt. 5. Serve the chops warm with the sauce.

Barbecue Pulled Beef

Prep Time: 20 minutes | Cook Time: 4 hours | Serves: 4

1 (3-pound) chuck roast
2 tablespoons salt, plus more for seasoning

2 tablespoons black pepper

1. Season the chuck roast with salt and pepper, covering the surface fully. 2. Set Traeger temperature to 300°F and preheat, lid closed for 15 minutes. 3. Place the roast on the grill. Close the lid and cook for 4 to 5 hours, turning once every hour. The roast is fully cooked when the meat reaches an internal temperature of 180°F and feels tender (with no resistance) when probed with a metal skewer or meat thermometer. 4. Let the roast rest for 10 to 15 minutes. Using two large forks, pull apart the beef. Taste and season with more salt to taste and serve immediately.

Flavorful Pepper Steak Stir-Fry

Prep Time: 25 minutes | Cook Time: 5 minutes | Serves: 6

Sauce:
½ cup low-sodium beef broth
¼ cup oyster sauce
2 tablespoons low-sodium soy sauce
1 tablespoon granulated sugar
2 teaspoons cornstarch
1 tablespoon vegetable oil
1 tablespoon toasted sesame oil
1 tablespoon peeled, finely grated fresh ginger

2 large garlic cloves, minced or pushed through a press
1-pound top sirloin, cut into strips about 3 inches by ¼ inch by ¼ inch
3 large bell peppers, 1 red, 1 green, 1 orange, each cut into ¼-inch strips
1 medium yellow onion, cut vertically in half and thinly sliced
¼ cup fresh cilantro leaves
3 cups cooked rice

1. Whisk the sauce ingredients. 2. Whisk the vegetable oil, sesame oil, ginger, and garlic. Add the sirloin strips and turn to coat. 3. Set Traeger temperature to 500°F and preheat, lid closed for 15 minutes. 4. Place a grill-proof wok on the grill grate, close the lid, and preheat it for about 10 minutes. Bring the sauce, top sirloin mixture, bell peppers, onion, and cilantro to the grill and keep close by. 5. When the wok is smoking hot, add the top sirloin mixture, separating the meat as you add it to the wok. Grill the meat with the lid open, until the meat starts to brown and releases easily from the wok, about 1 minute, stirring once after 30 seconds. Add the bell peppers and the onion all at once. Stir to combine and cook until the vegetables turn a shade brighter, about 2 minutes, stirring frequently. Add the sauce, stir for 10 seconds, close the lid, and cook until the sauce comes to a boil, about 1 minute. Simmer until the sauce is thick enough to coat the vegetables, about 1 minute more. Stir in the cilantro. 6. Remove the wok from the grill and serve the stir-fry immediately over warm rice.

Thyme Flank Steak with Balsamic Pearl Onions

Prep Time: 15 minutes | Cook Time: 30 minutes | Serves: 4

¾ cup water
½ cup balsamic vinegar
2 tablespoons honey
1½ teaspoons tomato paste
1 large bay leaf
1 package (14 ounces) frozen pearl onions, thawed

3½ teaspoons finely chopped fresh thyme leaves, divided
2 teaspoons kosher salt, divided
1 teaspoon freshly ground black pepper, divided
1 flank steak, about 1½ pounds and ¾ inch thick
1 tablespoon extra-virgin olive oil
Fresh thyme sprigs (optional)

1. In a large skillet, combine the water, vinegar, honey, tomato paste, and bay leaf. Add the onions and bring to a simmer over medium-low heat. Cover and simmer for 10 minutes, stirring occasionally. Uncover the skillet and increase the heat to high. Boil until the liquid starts to thicken and is reduced to 4 to 5 tablespoons, about 5 minutes. Remove from the heat and stir in 1½ teaspoons of the thyme, 1 teaspoon of the salt, and ½ teaspoon of the pepper. The sauce will continue to thicken as it cools. If necessary, add water, 1 tablespoon at a time, to thin the mixture to your desired consistency. 2. Combine the remaining 2 teaspoons thyme, 1 teaspoon salt, and ½ teaspoon pepper. Brush the steak on both sides with the oil and season evenly with the spice mixture, pressing the spices into the meat. Allow the steak to stand at room temperature for 15 to 30 minutes before grilling. 3. Set Traeger temperature to 400°F and preheat, lid closed for 15 minutes. 4. Place the steak on the grill grate, with the lid closed, until cooked to your desired doneness, 8 to 10 minutes for medium rare, turning once or twice. Remove from the grill and let rest for 3 to 5 minutes. Cut the steak across the grain into thin slices. Serve immediately with the onions and their sauce. Garnish with thyme, if using.

Korean-Inspired Short Ribs

Prep Time: 20 minutes | Cook Time: 8 minutes | Serves: 4

4 pounds boneless beef short ribs
1 cup packed light brown sugar
½ cup soy sauce
⅓ cup water
¼ cup mirin (rice wine)

1 small onion, minced
1 small pear, grated
¼ cup minced garlic
2 tablespoons sesame oil
¼ teaspoon black pepper

1. Cut the beef. Using a sharp knife, cut the beef lengthwise into ¼-inch strips. 2. In a medium bowl, whisk the brown sugar, soy sauce, water, mirin, onion, pear, garlic, sesame oil, and pepper until combined. Put the beef in a gallon-size resealable bag and pour the marinade over it. Seal the bag, removing all the air. Refrigerate to marinate for 1 to 4 hours. 3. Set Traeger temperature to 400°F and preheat, lid closed for 15 minutes. 4. Remove the short ribs from the marinade and place them on the grill grate. Discard the marinade. Cook, uncovered, for 4 to 5 minutes per side, turning frequently, until the beef reaches an internal temperature of about 135°F. 5. Let the beef rest for 5 minutes, then serve immediately.

Garlic Beef Tenderloin with Romesco Sauce

Prep Time: 10 minutes | Cook Time: 1½ hours | Serves: 10

½ cup roasted red peppers
⅓ cup natural almonds
2 tablespoons red wine vinegar
½ teaspoon red pepper flakes
2 cloves garlic, peeled
1 slice sourdough bread, crust removed
¼ cup extra-virgin olive oil

1 whole beef tenderloin (about 6½ pounds), silver skin removed (it's best to have your butcher remove this; unless you have a super-sharp knife, you're likely to lose some of the meat along with the silver skin)
6 cloves garlic, thinly sliced
Kosher salt and freshly ground black pepper
12 green onions, trimmed

1. Place the roasted peppers, almonds, vinegar, red pepper flakes, whole garlic cloves, and bread in a blender and pulse to combine. With the machine running, add the oil slowly and process until you have a nice thick sauce. The Romesco sauce can be prepared a day ahead and refrigerated in an airtight container. Bring to room temperature before using. 2. Using a boning knife, cut small slits into the beef tenderloin and slide in the slices of garlic. Liberally season with salt and pepper. Let rest at room temperature for at least 45 minutes before cooking. 3. Set Traeger temperature to 500°F and preheat, lid closed for 15 minutes. 4. Place the tenderloin on the grill, close the lid, and sear for 5 minutes per side. 5. Put the tenderloin on a rack in a roasting pan and put the pan on the grill. Throw the green onions on the grill as well. Close the lid. Adjust the temperature to 400°F and continue to roast to your desired degree of doneness, 1 hour to 1 hour and 15 minutes for medium rare (an internal temperature of 135° to 140° F). 6. Transfer the tenderloin to a platter and let rest for at least 15 minutes. To serve, slice, arrange the green onions with the beef, and spoon the Romesco sauce over everything. This is delicious warm or at room temperature.

California French Beef Roast

Prep Time: 10 minutes | Cook Time: 1⬚ hours | Serves: 6

1 (3-pound) boneless chuck roast
1 (16-ounce) bottle California French dressing
Kosher salt and freshly ground black pepper

1 tablespoon honey
1 tablespoon chopped fresh chives
Pumpernickel bread for serving (optional)

1. Place the roast in a 1-gallon zip-top plastic bag. Pour off ¼ cup of the dressing and set it aside. Pour the rest of the bottle into the bag. Seal the bag and squish the dressing around the roast to coat it completely. Refrigerate for up to 24 hours. 2. Remove the roast from the bag and discard the marinade. Season liberally with salt and pepper. Let stand at room temperature for 30 minutes. 3. Set Traeger temperature to 500°F and preheat, lid closed for 15 minutes. 4. Place the roast on the grill, close the lid, and sear for 5 minutes per side. Remove the roast from the grill. 5. Put the roast on a rack in a roasting pan and put the pan on the grill. Close the lid and adjust the temperature to 375°F. Roast until the internal temperature at the thickest point is 175° F, about 1½ hours. 6. Transfer the roast to a cutting board. Drizzle with the honey and sprinkle with the chives. Let rest for 15 minutes, then slice thinly across the grain. Serve on a platter or make sandwiches with it using the pumpernickel bread.

Garlic New York Strip Roast

Prep Time: 10 minutes | Cook Time: 1½ hours | Serves: 8

1 tablespoon Canadian-Style Steak Seasoning
1 tablespoon garlic paste (about 8 cloves garlic, smashed and worked into a paste, or prepared garlic paste in a tube, which can be found in the produce section)

1 tablespoon Worcestershire sauce
1 teaspoon Dijon mustard
1 (3- to 4-pound) New York strip loin roast
Horseradish or steak sauce for serving

1. In a small bowl, combine the steak seasoning, garlic, Worcestershire, and mustard and massage the mixture into the roast. Set the roast on a rack in a roasting pan and let stand at room temperature for an hour. 2. Set Traeger temperature to 450°F and preheat, lid closed for 15 minutes. 3. Put the roast on the grill grate. Close the lid and cook to your desired degree of doneness, 1½ to 2 hours for medium rare (an internal temperature of 135° to 140° F). 4. Transfer the roast to a cutting board and let rest for 15 minutes. Slice as you prefer (I like ½-inch-thick slices), arrange on a platter, and serve with the sauces if desired.

Horseradish-Crusted Rib Roast with Butter Gravy

Prep Time: 20 minutes | Cook Time: 1 hour 15 minutes | Serves: 8

1 (5- to 6-pound) bone-in standing rib roast, trimmed of excess fat
6 large cloves garlic, peeled
¼ cup grated, peeled fresh horseradish or well-drained prepared horseradish
2 tablespoons chopped fresh oregano
1 tablespoon chopped fresh rosemary
1 tablespoon kosher salt

1 tablespoon freshly ground black pepper
¼ cup extra-virgin olive oil
½ cup dry white wine
1 tablespoon gravy flour or all-purpose flour
2 cups low-sodium chicken broth
2 sprigs fresh thyme
¼ cup (½ stick) unsalted butter, cut into tablespoons

1. Let the roast stand at room temperature 30 to 45 minutes.
2. In a mini food processor or blender, finely mince the garlic, horseradish, oregano, rosemary, salt, and pepper together. Add the olive oil all at once and process into a paste. Smear the paste all over the roast. Set the roast on a rack in a roasting pan and let sit at room temperature for another hour. 3. Set Traeger temperature to 450°F and preheat, lid closed for 15 minutes. 4. Place the roasting pan on the grill grate, close the lid, and roast for 45 minutes. 5. Adjust the grill temperature to 350°F and roast for another 30 minutes, or cook until it has an internal temperature of 125° to 130° F. As soon as you hit it, remove the roast from the grill. 6. Transfer the roast to a cutting board, loosely tent with aluminum foil, and let rest for 20 to 30 minutes. The internal temperature will rise 5 to 10 degrees. 7. Meanwhile, pour off some of the fat and place the pan over two burners on the stove set at medium heat. Pour in the wine and scrape up the browned bits from the bottom of the pan. 8. Whisk in the flour, then whisk in the broth and add the thyme. Cook, stirring, until the gravy reaches the thickness you like. Remove the pan from the heat and whisk in the butter. 9. Carve meat into slices and serve with the pan gravy.

Caramelizd Beef Slices

Prep Time: 30 minutes | Cook Time: 6 minutes | Serves: 4

1-pound rib eye steak
½ cup soy sauce
2 tablespoons minced garlic

2 tablespoons toasted sesame oil
2 tablespoons plum syrup
2 teaspoons coarse ground black pepper

1. Freeze the steak for about 30 minutes to make it easier to handle. Once it is frozen, slice the steak across the grain into thin, even pieces, about ⅛ inch thick. 2. In a medium bowl, whisk together the soy sauce, garlic, oil, plum syrup, and pepper. Add the sliced beef and combine until the marinade is evenly incorporated. Cover and refrigerate the bowl and let the beef marinate for at least 4 hours, although 24 hours is best. 3. Set Traeger temperature to 500°F and preheat, lid closed for 15 minutes. 4. When you're ready to grill, shake off and discard any excess marinade from the beef. Grill the meat for about 3 minutes per side, until you start to see caramelization. Don't overcrowd the bulgogi or the meat will steam instead of sear.

Grilled Hot Dogs with Spicy Pickled Vegetables

Prep Time: 20 minutes | Cook Time: 6 minutes | Serves: 6

4 cups roughly chopped, tightly packed (½-inch pieces) green cabbage
2 Kirby or Persian cucumbers, seeded and cut into ½-inch dice
1 medium yellow onion, chopped
½ red bell pepper, cut into ½-inch dice
2 jalapeño chile peppers, seeded and finely chopped
1 tablespoon kosher salt

1 cup cider vinegar
⅔ cup packed golden brown sugar
1 teaspoon mustard powder
½ teaspoon celery seed
¼ teaspoon ground turmeric
12 all-beef hot dogs
12 hot dog buns, split

1. In a large colander toss the cabbage, cucumbers, onion, bell pepper, jalapeños, and salt. Place a dinner plate on top of the vegetables to weigh them down. Let stand in the sink to drain for 1 hour. 2. In a large saucepan over medium heat, combine the vinegar, brown sugar, mustard powder, celery seed, and turmeric. Bring to a simmer, stirring to dissolve the sugar. Add the cabbage mixture (do not rinse) to the saucepan and cook until the cabbage is crisp-tender, 4 to 6 minutes, stirring occasionally. Transfer to a bowl and let cool for 2 hours at room temperature. Cover and refrigerate for at least 2 hours or up to 3 days. 3. Set Traeger temperature to 400°F and preheat, lid closed for 15 minutes. 4. Cut a few shallow slashes in each hot dog. Grill the hot dogs, with the lid closed, until lightly marked on the outside and hot all the way through, 5 to 7 minutes, turning occasionally. During the last minute of grilling time, toast the buns, cut side down on the grill grate. 5. Place the hot dogs in the buns. Using a slotted spoon to drain the excess liquid, spoon about ¼ cup of the vegetables on top of each hot dog. Serve immediately.

Parmesan Meatballs

Prep Time: 15 minutes | Cook Time: 55 minutes | Serves: 6

1-pound ground beef
½ cup Italian bread crumbs
4 garlic cloves, minced
1 egg

¼ cup grated Parmesan cheese
Kosher salt
Freshly ground black pepper

1. In a large bowl, combine the ground beef, bread crumbs, garlic, egg, Parmesan cheese, salt, and pepper. Mix together with your hands and roll the mixture into 1½-inch meatballs. 2. Set Traeger temperature to 225°F and preheat, lid closed for 15 minutes. 3. Once preheated, place the meatballs on the grill grates for 45 minutes. Turn the temperature up to 450°F for 10 to 15 minutes, or until the meatballs reach an internal temperature of 165°F. You can flip them, if desired, during the last few minutes.

Grilled T-Bone Steaks with Moroccan Spice Paste

Prep Time: 15 minutes | Cook Time: 8 minutes | Serves: 4

4 T-bone steaks, each about 12 ounces and 1-inch-thick, trimmed of excess fat
Paste:
3 medjool dates, each cut into quarters
2 tablespoons red wine vinegar
¼ cup extra-virgin olive oil
1½ teaspoons kosher salt

1 teaspoon ground cumin
½ teaspoon smoked paprika
½ teaspoon ground ginger
½ teaspoon freshly ground black pepper

1. In a small bowl, combine the dates and the vinegar. Add just enough hot water to cover, and let stand until the dates are softened, about 10 minutes. Transfer the mixture to a food processor, add the remaining paste ingredients, and process until smooth. 2. Set aside 3 tablespoons of the paste in a small bowl. Spread the remaining paste evenly on both sides of each steak. Allow the steaks to stand at room temperature for 15 to 30 minutes before grilling. 3. Set Traeger temperature to 500°F and preheat, lid closed for 15 minutes. 4. Grill the steaks with the lid closed, until cooked to your desired doneness, 6 to 8 minutes for medium rare, turning once or twice. Remove from the grill and brush the top of the steaks with the reserved paste. Let rest for 3 to 5 minutes. Serve warm.

Chapter 5 Pork Recipes

63 Aromatic Baby Back Ribs

63 Spicy Pork Sandwiches With Apple-Onion Chutney

64 Lemon Pork Kebabs

64 Texas Pork Steaks

64 Rosemary Pork Loin Chops with Pear

65 Mexican Pork Loin Roast

65 Bacon-Wrapped Sausage Fatty

65 Barbecue Pork Riblets

66 Brined Bone-In Pork Loin

66 Grilled Sausage Olive Pizzas

67 Mango-Ginger Glazed Baby Back Ribs

67 Maple-Bourbon Pork Chops with Applesauce

67 Homemade Pork Belly Bacon

68 Savory Pork Sliders with Black Bean Salsa

68 Cheese Pepperoni Mushroom Pizza

69 Fresh Huevos Rancheros

69 Vietnamese Pork Noodle

69 Pulled Pork Stew

70 Lime Spareribs with Adobo and Garlic Butter

70 Greek Pork Souvlaki

70 Teriyaki Pork Tenderloin

71 Flavorful Roasted Suckling Pig

71 BBQ Pulled Pork

72 Citrus Pork Butt

72 Juicy Pork Chops

Aromatic Baby Back Ribs

Prep Time: 30 minutes | Cook Time: 4 hours | Serves: 6

For the Spice Rub:

3 tablespoons cumin seeds, whole

3 tablespoons coriander seeds, whole

3 tablespoons fennel seeds, whole

1 tablespoon allspice berries, whole

3 tablespoons paprika

3 tablespoons chili powder

1 tablespoon garlic powder

1 tablespoon onion powder

For the Baby Back Ribs:

8 pounds baby back pork ribs, trimmed and membranes removed

Flaked sea salt

Freshly ground black pepper

2 cups packed dark brown sugar

2 cups dark molasses

2 cups wildflower honey

2 cups apple cider

½ cup bourbon (or brandy)

To make the spice rub: 1. Preheat a heavy-bottom pan over medium heat on the stovetop. 2. Combine the cumin, coriander, fennel, and allspice. Toast the spices for about 5 minutes, until they're fragrant and smoky, gently tossing them to toast evenly. Let cool slightly. Grind the spices in a mortar with a pestle or in a clean spice or coffee grinder until smooth. Transfer to a small bowl. 3. Stir in the paprika, chili powder, garlic powder, and onion powder. Store in an airtight container.

To make the baby back ribs: 1. Set Traeger temperature to 250°F and preheat, lid closed for 15 minutes. 2. Rub the spice mixture evenly over both sides of the ribs. Season them with salt and pepper. Arrange the ribs on the grill grate, flesh-side up, leaving space between them. Smoke the ribs for about 2 hours; the meat will begin to shrink from the bones. 3. On a large sheet of aluminum foil, prepare a bed of brown sugar drizzled with the molasses and honey. 4. Place the ribs, flesh-side down, onto the sugar bed. Add the apple cider and bourbon. Tightly wrap the ribs in the foil and return them to the grill. Smoke for about 2 hours more. Remove the ribs from the grill and let rest for 20 minutes. 5. Unwrap the foil, remove the ribs, and serve with the sauce that developed in the foil.

Spicy Pork Sandwiches With Apple-Onion Chutney

Prep Time: 30 minutes | Cook Time: 10 hours | Serves: 8

For the Spice Rub:

3 tablespoons paprika

3 tablespoons chili powder

3 tablespoons ground chipotle pepper

3 tablespoons ground ancho chile pepper

1 tablespoon garlic powder

1 tablespoon onion powder

For the Pork Shoulder and Apple-Onion Chutney:

1 (8- to 10-pound) bone-in pork shoulder, trimmed

Flaked sea salt

Freshly ground black pepper

1 tablespoon unsalted butter

1 tablespoon canola oil

8 shallots, thinly sliced

4 Golden Delicious apples, cored, peeled, and cut into 8 wedges

4 thyme sprigs, leaves stripped and finely chopped

2 cups apple cider

2 cups hard cider

Pretzel buns, for serving

Whole-grain mustard, for serving

To make the spice rub: 1. In a small bowl, stir together the paprika, chili powder, chipotle pepper, ancho chile pepper, garlic powder, and onion powder until blended.

To make the pork shoulder and apple-onion chutney: 1. Set Traeger temperature to 250°F and preheat, lid closed for 15 minutes. 2. Preheat a large cast iron pan on the grill grate. 3. Evenly rub the spice mixture over all sides of the pork shoulder. Season it with salt and pepper. Place the pork in a shallow pan on the grill grate (the pan will collect the cooking liquid). Insert a probe thermometer (if available) into the thickest part of the meat, not touching the bone. Set the target temperature for 190°F. Smoke for about 4 hours; the meat will begin to shrink from the bones. 4. In the preheated cast iron pan, combine the butter, canola oil, shallots, apples, and thyme. Season with salt and pepper. 5. Remove the pan with the pork shoulder from the grill, then remove the pork from the pan. Collect the cooking liquid from the pan and strain it through a fine-mesh sieve set over a bowl. Using an injection needle, inject the shoulder with the liquid. Space your injections evenly around the shoulder. Place the shoulder back in the grill. Give the apples and shallots a quick toss. Smoke for 4 to 6 hours, tossing the chutney occasionally. 6. When the apples and shallots are tender, stir in the apple cider and hard cider to deglaze the pan, scraping up any browned bits from the bottom. Continue to cook the apples and shallots until your desired consistency is reached. Remove and set aside. 7. Once the internal temperature of the pork reaches 190°F, remove the pork and loosely tent it with aluminum foil. Let it rest for 1 hour. Using two forks, shred the pork. 8. Build your sandwich by layering the buns with pork, topped with apple-onion chutney and mustard.

Lemon Pork Kebabs

Prep Time: 25 minutes | Cook Time: 1½ hours | Serves: 5

1 cup ketchup
½ cup soy sauce
½ cup lemon-lime soda
Juice of 1 lemon
2 garlic cloves, minced
2 tablespoons olive oil

1 tablespoon sriracha
1 tablespoon white sugar
1 teaspoon onion powder
½ teaspoon salt
½ teaspoon freshly ground black pepper
1 (3-pound) pork butt or pork tenderloin

1. In a large nonreactive bowl, combine the ketchup, soy sauce, soda, lemon juice, garlic, olive oil, sriracha, sugar, onion powder, salt, and black pepper. Reserve ¾ cup of the marinade for basting. 2. Trim away excess fat from the pork and cut it into 1¼-inch cubes. Place the pork into the bowl with the marinade and toss to coat. Cover the bowl tightly with plastic wrap, and refrigerate for 6 to 10 hours. If using wooden skewers, soak them in tepid water 30 minutes before using. 3. Set Traeger temperature to 250°F and preheat, lid closed for 15 minutes. 4. Remove the pork from the refrigerator and discard the excess marinade. Thread the pork onto skewers, about 5 pieces per skewer. 5. Place the skewers into the grill, close the lid, and cook for 1½ to 2 hours, turning the kebabs after 1 hour. During the last 30 minutes of cook time, baste the skewers with the reserved marinade. 6. Once the internal temperature of the kebabs reaches 155°F, remove from the grill and let them rest for 10 minutes before serving.

Texas Pork Steaks

Prep Time: 20 minutes | Cook Time: 2-3 hours | Serves: 4

½ cup brown sugar
2 tablespoons kosher salt
1 tablespoon chili powder
2 teaspoons freshly ground black pepper

1 teaspoon onion powder
4 (1-inch-thick) pork steaks
½ cup apple juice

1. Set Traeger temperature to 250°F and preheat, lid closed for 15 minutes. 2. In a small bowl, combine the brown sugar, salt, chili powder, pepper, and onion powder. Apply the rub liberally to both sides and edges of the pork steaks. 3. Place the pork steaks right on the grill grate. Close the lid and cook for 1 hour. 4. Pour the apple juice into a spray bottle. After 1 hour of cooking, spritz the steaks with the apple juice. Continue to cook, spritzing every 30 minutes, until they reach an internal temperature of between 180°F and 185°F, about 1½ to 2 hours. 5. Remove the steaks, let them rest for 10 to 15 minutes, and serve.

Rosemary Pork Loin Chops with Pear

Prep Time: 20 minutes | Cook Time: 1½ hours | Serves: 4

1 tablespoon extra-virgin olive oil, plus more for brushing
1 tablespoon unsalted butter
4 bone-in pork chops
2 tablespoons flaked sea salt
Freshly ground black pepper

¼ cup smoked paprika
8 rosemary sprigs
2 Bosc or Bartlett pears, halved and cored
2 limes, halved

1. Set Traeger temperature to 275°F and preheat, lid closed for 15 minutes. 2. Preheat a large cast iron skillet on the grill grate, then pour in the olive oil and add the butter to melt. 3. Brush the pork chops all over with olive oil. Season with salt, pepper, and paprika. Press 2 rosemary sprigs into the oiled surface of each chop. 4. Place the chops, rosemary-side down, on the grill grate. Insert a probe thermometer (if available) into the thickest part of the meat, not touching the bone. Set the target temperature for 145°F. Smoke for 1 to 1½ hours until the internal temperature reaches 145°F. 5. Place the pears in the skillet, flesh-side down. Cook for about 20 minutes, until tender. Remove and set aside. 6. Transfer the pork to a cutting board. Loosely tent it with aluminum foil and let it rest for 10 minutes. 7. Serve the chops topped with any of the liquid that accumulated while resting, a thinly sliced pear, and half a lime for squeezing.

Mexican Pork Loin Roast

Prep Time: 10 minutes | Cook Time: 1 hour | Serves: 6

2 tablespoons chili powder
2 tablespoons light brown sugar
1 teaspoon ground cumin
½ teaspoon ground cinnamon
1 teaspoon dried oregano
1 teaspoon paprika

1 teaspoon garlic powder
1½ teaspoons salt
¾ teaspoon black pepper
1 (3-pound) pork loin roast
3 tablespoons olive oil

1. In a small bowl, stir together the chili powder, brown sugar, cumin, cinnamon, oregano, paprika, garlic powder, salt, and pepper to blend. Lightly coat the pork with olive oil, then sprinkle the seasoning mixture evenly over the pork, covering all surfaces. Put the pork on a plate, cover, and let sit at room temperature for 1 hour. 2. Set Traeger temperature to 300°F and preheat, lid closed for 15 minutes. 3. Place the pork on the grill grate. Close the lid and cook for about 1 hour, or until the pork reaches an internal temperature of 140°F. Transfer the pork to a plate. 4. Let the pork rest for 10 minutes, then cut it into ½-inch-thick slices. Serve immediately.

Bacon-Wrapped Sausage Fatty

Prep Time: 20 minutes | Cook Time: 2 hours | Serves: 4

8 thin-cut bacon slices
1-pound ground breakfast sausage
½ cup grated pepper Jack cheese

1 jalapeño pepper, finely chopped
½ cup grated cheddar cheese

1. On a 12- to 18-inch piece of plastic wrap, lay out the bacon slices horizontally. On another piece of plastic wrap, place the ground sausage in the center. Place a piece of plastic wrap over the sausage and roll it into an 8-by-8-inch square. Remove the top piece of plastic wrap and carefully flip the sausage onto the bacon strips. Remove the plastic wrap that's now on top. Evenly spread the pepper Jack cheese, jalapeño, and cheddar cheese over the sausage. Using the bottom piece of plastic wrap to help, roll the sausage tightly, with the filling inside, into a log. 2. Set Traeger temperature to 300°F and preheat, lid closed for 15 minutes. 3. Place the fatty on the grill grate. Close the lid and cook for 2 hours, turning once every 30 minutes. The fatty is fully cooked when the internal temperature reaches 165°F. 4. Let the fatty rest for 10 to 15 minutes. Cut it into ½-inch slices, or as desired, and serve immediately.

Barbecue Pork Riblets

Prep Time: 15 minutes | Cook Time: 2 hours | Serves: 5

For the Riblets:
2½ pounds pork riblets
¼ cup Dijon mustard (use more if needed)
For the Sauce:
½ cup ketchup
½ cup apple jelly
¼ cup water
¼ cup apple cider vinegar
¼ cup dark brown sugar

2 tablespoons plus 2 teaspoons All-Purpose Rub

1 teaspoon All-Purpose Rub
1 tablespoon blackstrap molasses
½ teaspoon Worcestershire sauce
1 tablespoon butter

1. Set Traeger temperature to 250°F and preheat, lid closed for 15 minutes. 2. Coat each riblet section with Dijon mustard. Then season the riblets on both sides with the All-Purpose Rub. 3. Place the riblets on the grill grate, close the lid, and cook for about 1 hour, or until the riblets reach an internal temperature of between 175°F and 180°F, before saucing. 4. Meanwhile, in a small saucepan over medium-high heat, combine the ketchup, apple jelly, water, apple cider vinegar, brown sugar, and All-Purpose Rub and simmer for 1 minute. Reduce the heat to medium-low, and simmer for 5 minutes, stirring occasionally. Add the molasses and Worcestershire sauce, and simmer for 2 more minutes. Reduce the heat to low, if needed. Add the butter and stir until melted. Remove from heat, cover, and set aside. 5. After 1 hour of cooking, baste the riblets with the sauce every 15 minutes during the remaining hour of cook time. 6. Once the riblets reach an internal temperature of 195°F, they are done. Remove from the grill, let them rest for about 10 minutes, and serve as is, or slice into individual riblets.

Brined Bone-In Pork Loin

Prep Time: 20 minutes | Cook Time: 3½ hours | Serves: 8

1 (4- to 5-pound) bone-in pork loin (you may have to order this from your butcher in advance)

Brine:

¾ cup kosher salt

¼ cup firmly packed light brown sugar

12 cups water

¼ cup fennel seeds

½ cup black peppercorns

2 tablespoons slightly cracked juniper berries

Rub:

¾ cup fresh sage leaves

⅓ cup firmly packed light brown sugar

¼ cup kosher salt

¾ teaspoon ground fennel seeds

2 tablespoons kosher salt

2 tablespoons olive oil

8 cloves garlic, peeled

Glaze:

¾ cup cider vinegar

⅓ cup red currant jam

1 tablespoon dry mustard, like Colman's

1 tablespoon fennel seeds

1. Lightly score the fat on the loin in a 1-inch crosshatch pattern. 2. In a medium saucepan, combine the salt, brown sugar, and 4 cups of the water and bring to a boil. Stir until the salt and sugar dissolve completely. Remove from the heat and stir in the fennel, peppercorns, and juniper berries, then stir in the remaining 8 cups water. Transfer the brine to a container large enough to hold the brine and pork loin. Let the brine cool completely. Once cooled, add the pork loin and refrigerate at least 12 hours and no more than 24 hours. 3. Combine the rub ingredients in a food processor and pulse until mostly smooth and paste-like. 4. Remove the pork from the brine and pat dry. Spread the rub over it and let sit for 1 hour before smoking to come to room temperature. 5. Set Traeger temperature to 200°F and preheat, lid closed for 15 minutes. 6. Set the loin on the grill, close the lid, and smoke for 1 hour. 7. Meanwhile, combine the glaze ingredients in a small saucepan and simmer over medium heat, stirring occasionally, until the liquid is reduced by half and the mixture is syrupy. Transfer to a bowl until ready to use. 8. After an hour, brush the loin generously with the glaze and close the lid. Baste once more with the glaze after another 30 minutes, close the lid, and let smoke until the internal temperature reaches 145° F, about 2½ hours total time. If the loin takes on too much color before it's done cooking, tent with aluminum foil. 9. Transfer the loin to a cutting board and baste once more with the glaze. Let it rest for 30 minutes before carving. Serve warm or at room temperature.

Grilled Sausage Olive Pizzas

Prep Time: 30 minutes | Cook Time: 20 minutes | Serves: 8

2 balls (each about 1 pound) premade pizza dough

Extra-virgin olive oil

1 medium red or green bell pepper, cut into ¼-inch strips

½ small yellow onion, thinly sliced

8 ounces mild or spicy Italian sausage

All-purpose flour

1 can (8 ounces) tomato sauce

¼ cup thinly sliced black olives

2 tablespoons finely chopped fresh Italian parsley leaves

1 tablespoon finely chopped fresh thyme leaves

2 teaspoons finely chopped fresh rosemary leaves

1½ cups shredded mozzarella cheese

1. Remove the balls of dough from the refrigerator, if necessary, about 1 hour before grilling so that the dough is easier to roll. 2. In a large skillet over medium-high heat, warm 1 tablespoon oil. Add the bell pepper and the onion and cook until softened but not browned, about 3 minutes, stirring occasionally. Remove the vegetables from the skillet and set aside. 3. Add the sausage to the skillet, breaking it into medium-sized pieces. Cook over medium-high heat until lightly browned and fully cooked, about 3 minutes, stirring occasionally and breaking the sausage into smaller pieces. Remove the skillet from the heat, and let the sausage cool in the skillet. 4. Set Traeger temperature to 400°F and preheat, lid closed for 15 minutes. 5. Meanwhile, prepare your first pizza. Using a rolling pin on a lightly floured work surface, roll out the dough, one ball at a time, into rounds about 12 inches wide and ⅓ inch thick. (If the dough retracts, cover it with a kitchen towel, let it rest for 5 minutes, and then continue.) Set the first round aside while you roll out the second. 6. Carefully transfer your first round of pizza dough onto a pizza peel (or a rimless baking sheet) lightly coated with flour. Spread ½ cup of the sauce over the dough. Scatter half of the sausage, half of the pepper-and-onion mixture, half of the olives, and half of the parsley, thyme, and rosemary on top. Finish by scattering half of the cheese on top of everything. 7. Slide your first pizza onto the preheated grill grate, with the lid closed, until the crust is golden brown and the cheese is melted, 9 to 11 minutes. Using a pizza peel or a large spatula, remove the pizza from the grill and let rest for a few minutes. Cut into wedges and serve warm.

Mango-Ginger Glazed Baby Back Ribs

Prep Time: 1 hour | Cook Time: 3 hours | Serves: 8

2 racks of baby back ribs
Kosher salt

Freshly ground black pepper
1 cup Mango-Ginger Rib Glaze

1. Set Traeger temperature to 250°F and preheat, lid closed for 15 minutes. 2. Using a butter knife, loosen the membrane on the back of the rib rack at one of the corners. Grab the loose end with a paper towel and give it a good pull. 3. Season both sides of the ribs with a few pinches of salt and pepper. 4. Place the ribs bone-down on the grill grate and close the lid. 5.Check the ribs for tenderness about 3 to 3½ hours into the cook. You want to see a little "pullback" on the ribs. You should be able to push a toothpick or meat probe into the meat between the bones and pull it out with very little resistance. 5. About 30 minutes before the end of your cook, baste the ribs with the glaze until it "sets" and becomes very sticky. 6. Remove the ribs from the grill and allow them to rest, loosely covered, for about 20 minutes before cutting and serving.

Maple-Bourbon Pork Chops with Applesauce

Prep Time: 15 minutes | Cook Time: 42 minutes | Serves: 4

For the Applesauce:
1 (48-ounce) jar chunky no-sugar-added applesauce
1 teaspoon ground cinnamon
For the Pork Chops:
4 (5-ounce) pork loin chops (about 1 inch thick)
Canola oil
2 teaspoons kosher salt
2 teaspoons freshly ground black pepper

2 teaspoons dark brown sugar
1 teaspoon freshly squeezed lemon juice (optional)

2 tablespoons unsalted butter, at room temperature
3 tablespoons maple syrup
⅓ cup bourbon

1. Set Traeger temperature to 350°F and preheat, lid closed for 15 minutes. 2. In a disposable aluminum pan, stir together the applesauce, cinnamon, brown sugar, and lemon juice (if using). Place the pan on the grill, close the lid, and smoke for 20 minutes. 3. Meanwhile, pat the pork chops dry with a paper towel and lightly coat them with oil. Season the meat with salt and pepper. 4. In a small saucepan on the stovetop over medium-low heat, melt the butter and maple syrup. Carefully stir in the bourbon, turn the heat to medium and cook the glaze for 3-5 minutes or until it starts to reduce and thicken. Remove from the heat. 5. Remove the applesauce from the grill. 6. Place the pork chops on the grill, close the lid, and let the chops grill for 10 minutes. 7. Then brush the tops of the chops with the maple-bourbon sauce. Cook for 2 minutes, flip the chops, and glaze them. Continue this process, flipping and glazing every 2 minutes, for 4 to 6 minutes, or until the internal temperature of the pork reaches 145°F. 8. Remove the pork chops from the grill, cover loosely with aluminum foil, and let them rest for 5 minutes. Serve with the smoked applesauce and remaining maple-bourbon sauce on the side.

Homemade Pork Belly Bacon

Prep Time: 20 minutes | Cook Time: 2 hours | Serves: 12

4 pounds pork belly, skin removed
1 cup brown sugar
¼ cup plus 2 tablespoons kosher salt (or other coarse, non-

iodized salt)
2½ teaspoons coarsely ground black pepper
1 teaspoon curing salt (optional)

1. Trim away any loose pieces of meat or fat from the pork belly. It should be square and uniform in thickness. Pat it completely dry with paper towels. 2. In a medium bowl, combine the brown sugar, kosher salt, black pepper, and curing salt (if using). Mix well. 3. Coat the pork belly thickly with the mixture and place it into a large resealable bag. Refrigerate the pork for 7 to 9 days, turning it over once a day. 4. Set Traeger temperature to 200°F and preheat, lid closed for 15 minutes.
Rinse the pork belly completely to remove excess salt and sugar. Pat dry with paper towels. Place the pork belly on the grill grate. 5. Smoke for 2 hours, or until the internal temperature of the center of the pork belly reaches 150°F. 6. Remove from the grill and wrap in butcher paper and then plastic wrap. Place immediately in the refrigerator to cool for at least 2 hours before slicing. 7. Before you are ready to slice the bacon, place it in the freezer for 20 minutes. This will make it easier to cut thin, even slices.

Savory Pork Sliders with Black Bean Salsa

Prep Time: 20 minutes | Cook Time: 8 minutes | Serves: 6

Salsa:
1 can (15 ounces) black beans, rinsed and drained
¾ cup finely chopped green bell pepper
¼ cup coarsely grated red onion
2 tablespoons extra-virgin olive oil
2 tablespoons minced fresh cilantro leaves

1 tablespoon red wine vinegar
½ teaspoon dried oregano
¼ teaspoon hot pepper sauce, or to taste
¼ teaspoon smoked paprika
¼ teaspoon kosher salt

Patties:
1½ pounds lean ground pork
¼ cup coarsely grated red onion
1 teaspoon mustard powder
1 teaspoon dried oregano

1 teaspoon kosher salt
½ teaspoon smoked paprika
½ teaspoon freshly ground black pepper
12 small dinner rolls, split

1. Combine the salsa ingredients. Set aside. 2. Set Traeger temperature to 400°F and preheat, lid closed for 15 minutes. 3. Gently combine the patty ingredients. With wet hands form 12 loosely packed patties of equal size, each about 3 inches in diameter. Don't compact the meat too much or the patties will be tough. Using your thumb or the back of a spoon, make a shallow indentation about ½ inch wide in the center of each patty. This will help the patties cook evenly and prevent them from puffing on the grill. 4. Place the patties on the grill grate, with the lid closed, until fully cooked, 6 to 8 minutes, turning once or twice. During the last minute of grilling time, toast the rolls, cut side down, over direct heat. Remove from the grill and assemble the patties in the rolls with the salsa on top (you may have leftover salsa). Serve immediately.

Cheese Pepperoni Mushroom Pizza

Prep Time: 30 minutes | Cook Time: 55 minutes | Serves: 8

Filling:
1 tablespoon extra-virgin olive oil
3 cups finely chopped yellow onions
1½ cups diced green bell pepper
1-pound button mushrooms, sliced

4 large garlic cloves, minced or pushed through a press
1 teaspoon kosher salt
½ teaspoon freshly ground black pepper

Sauce:
1 can (8 ounces) tomato sauce
¼ cup freshly grated Parmigiano-Reggiano® cheese
2 tablespoons tomato paste
1 tablespoon extra-virgin olive oil
½ teaspoon dried oregano
½ teaspoon dried basil
1 garlic clove, minced or pushed through a press

¼ teaspoon dried thyme
Extra-virgin olive oil
1½ pounds premade pizza dough
All-purpose flour
7 ounces grated mozzarella cheese (about 2 cups)
5 ounces sliced pepperoni

1. In a large skillet over medium heat, warm the oil. Add the onions and bell pepper and cook until slightly softened, about 3 minutes, stirring occasionally. Add the mushrooms and cook until tender and lightly browned and any liquid they have released is evaporated, about 12 minutes. During the last minute, stir in the garlic, salt, and pepper. Remove the filling from the heat and set aside to cool. 2. Combine the sauce ingredients. Remove the dough from the refrigerator, if necessary, about 1 hour before grilling so that the dough is easier to roll. 3. Lightly coat a 10-inch cast-iron skillet with oil. Divide the dough into two balls, one with two-thirds of the dough and the other with the remaining one-third. On a lightly floured work surface, roll, pat, and stretch the larger ball into a 14-inch round. (If the dough retracts, cover it with a kitchen towel, let it rest for 5 minutes, and then continue rolling.) 4. Transfer the dough to the skillet, letting the excess hang over the sides to keep the dough from sliding into the skillet. Gently stretch the dough to fit the skillet, pressing it into the corners but being careful not to tear the dough. Spread 1 cup of the mozzarella on top of the dough. Spread one-half of the filling on top of the cheese and then place one-half of the pepperoni in a single layer on top of the filling. Repeat with another layer using the remaining filling and the remaining pepperoni. Top evenly with ½ cup of the mozzarella. Roll, pat, and stretch the remaining piece of dough into a 10-inch round. Place the round on top of the filling and press down to remove any visible air pockets. Brush some water on the edges of the top and bottom pieces of dough where they come together, and then roll and pinch the edges to seal them. 5. Prick the dough in several places to release any new air pockets that may have formed. Spread the sauce over the top crust, leaving the edges where the dough is sealed uncovered. Top the sauce with the remaining ½ cup mozzarella. 6. Set Traeger temperature to 400°F and preheat, lid closed for 15 minutes. 7. Place the skillet on the grill grate, close the lid, and cook until the edges of the dough look set and somewhat dry, about 40 minutes. Remove the skillet from the grill and let the pizza rest for 10 minutes. Using a wide spatula, slide the pizza onto a serving platter. Cut into wedges and serve warm.

Fresh Huevos Rancheros

Prep Time: 30 minutes | Cook Time: 40 minutes | Serves: 4

3 poblano chile peppers, about 14 ounces total
1½ teaspoons canola oil
12 ounces fresh chorizo sausages, casings removed
3 large garlic cloves, minced or pushed through a press
1 cup sliced scallions (white and light green parts only)
2 teaspoons ground cumin
1 can (28 ounces) diced plum tomatoes in juice

1 can (15 ounces) black beans, rinsed and drained
Kosher salt
Freshly ground black pepper
3 ½ ounces pepper jack cheese, coarsely grated
4 large eggs
8 corn tortillas (6 inches)

1. Set Traeger temperature to 500°F and preheat, lid closed for 15 minutes. 2. Place the poblanos on the grill grate, with the lid closed, until blackened and blistered all over, 10 to 12 minutes, turning occasionally. Put the poblanos in a bowl and cover with plastic wrap to trap the steam. Let stand for about 10 minutes. Peel away and discard the charred skin. Cut off and discard the stems and seeds, and then roughly chop the poblanos. 3. Place a 10-inch cast-iron skillet on the grill, add the oil, and warm for 1 minute. Add the chorizo and break into small pieces using a wooden spoon. Cook until the chorizo is lightly browned, 5 to 6 minutes, stirring occasionally. Stir in the garlic, scallions, and poblanos and cook for 2 to 3 minutes. Stir in the cumin, the tomatoes in juice, the beans, ½ teaspoon salt, and ½ teaspoon pepper. Bring to a boil and cook until the flavors are blended, the liquid is reduced by two-thirds, and only a small amount of liquid remains in the bottom of the skillet, 12 to 16 minutes, stirring occasionally. Top evenly with the cheese and cook until most of the cheese is melted, 3 to 4 minutes. Keep the lid closed as much as possible during grilling. 4. Make four shallow indentations in the chile-bean mixture. Crack one egg into each indentation. Continue cooking over direct high heat, with the lid closed, until the egg whites are set but the yolks are still soft and runny, 3 to 5 minutes. Season the eggs with salt and pepper. Carefully remove the skillet from the grill. 5. Put four tortillas in each of two foil packets. Warm the packets over direct high heat for about 1 minute, turning once. Serve the huevos rancheros with warm tortillas.

Vietnamese Pork Noodle

Prep Time: 15 minutes | Cook Time: 5 minutes | Serves: 4

7 ounces dried vermicelli noodles
1 recipe vietnamese lemongrass pork, sliced
2 cups bean sprouts
2 cups fresh cilantro leaves
1 cup shredded carrots

1 cup shredded daikon or jicama
1 cup shredded lettuce
½ cup vietnamese fish sauce dressing
½ cup roasted unsalted peanuts, chopped, for garnish

1. Bring a large saucepan of water to a boil over high heat on the stove top. 2. Add the noodles. Cook according to the package directions. Drain thoroughly. 3. Divide the noodles, pork, bean sprouts, cilantro, carrots, daikon, lettuce, and dressing among four bowls. Toss to coat with the dressing, then top with the peanuts. Serve immediately.

Pulled Pork Stew

Prep Time: 5 minutes | Cook Time: 40 minutes | Serves: 10

2 tablespoons unsalted butter
1 large onion, diced
1 (28-ounce) can crushed tomatoes
4 cups carolina pulled pork
1 cup corn kernels
4 cups diced (1-inch) red or white potatoes (about 1 pound)
1 (15-ounce) can pinto beans, drained and rinsed

1-pound okra, stemmed and cut into ½-inch rounds
2 cups low-sodium chicken broth
1 tablespoon kosher salt
1 tablespoon freshly ground black pepper
1 tablespoon sweet paprika
1 tablespoon dried oregano
1 teaspoon cayenne pepper

1. Set Traeger temperature to 350°F and preheat a 5-quart cast iron Dutch oven on the grate with the grill lid closed. 2. Put the butter in the Dutch oven and close the grill lid. When melted, add the onion and stir to coat with the butter. Close the grill lid and cook for 8 to 10 minutes or until softened and browned. 3. Add the tomatoes, pork, corn, potatoes, beans, okra, broth, salt, pepper, paprika, oregano, and cayenne and stir to combine. Cover the Dutch oven with a tight-fitting lid, close the grill lid, and bring to a boil. 4. Reduce the grill temperature to 400°F. Remove the lid from the Dutch oven. Close the grill lid and cook, stirring occasionally, for 20 to 25 minutes or until thickened and the flavors meld. Serve immediately.

Lime Spareribs with Adobo and Garlic Butter

Prep Time: 10 minutes | Cook Time: 2 hours | Serves: 4

6 ancho chiles (about 2 ounces)
6 cloves garlic, chopped
Grated zest of 1 lime
¼ cup fresh lime juice (about 3 limes)
1 tablespoon maple syrup (grade B preferred)

2 teaspoons dried oregano
Kosher salt and freshly ground black pepper
1 (4- to 5-pound) rack of spareribs
1 cup (2 sticks) unsalted butter, softened
4 cloves garlic, finely chopped

1. Fill a 3-quart saucepan halfway with water. Bring to a boil, add the chiles, remove from the heat, and let steep until the chiles are soft and flexible, about 1 hour. 2. Drain the chiles, reserving 1 cup of the soaking water, then remove the stems and seeds from the chiles. Place the chiles in a blender along with the garlic, lime zest and juice, maple syrup, oregano, and the reserved soaking water. Blend until smooth and season to taste with salt and pepper. 3. Remove the membrane from the bone side of the ribs by grabbing it with a kitchen towel and ripping it off, then cut the rack in half. Place the ribs in a 2½-gallon zip-top plastic bag and add the marinade. Seal the bag and refrigerate for 4 hours, turning the bag once. 4. Set Traeger temperature to 200°F and preheat, lid closed for 15 minutes. 5. Place the ribs in the grill, close the lid, and smoke until the racks bend immediately when picked up with tongs, 2 to 2½ hours. 6. While the ribs are smoking, make the garlic butter. Using a fork, mash the softened butter with the finely chopped garlic in a small bowl until well mixed. Cover and refrigerate until needed. 7. When the ribs are done, transfer the racks to a baking sheet and rub the garlic butter liberally over the ribs. Cut into portions and drizzle any melted butter from the pan over the ribs. Serve immediately.

Greek Pork Souvlaki

Prep Time: 30 minutes | Cook Time: 8 minutes | Serves: 4

½ Cup Greek yogurt
1 teaspoon olive oil
1 tablespoon kosher salt

1 tablespoon dried oregano
Juice of ½ lemon
1½ pounds boneless pork loin, cut into 1-inch dice

1. In a large bowl, stir together the yogurt, oil, salt, oregano, and lemon juice. 2. Add the pork; toss to coat thoroughly. Refrigerate overnight. 3. Set Traeger temperature to 500°F and preheat, lid closed for 15 minutes. 4. If using wooden skewers, soak them in water for 30 minutes. 5. Shake off any excess marinade, and thread the pork onto the skewers. 6. Put the skewers on the grill grate. Close the lid and cook, turning halfway, for 6 to 8 minutes total or until grill marks appear and the pork is just cooked through. Serve immediately.

Teriyaki Pork Tenderloin

Prep Time: 20 minutes | Cook Time: 5 hours | Serves: 6

1 (2½- to 3-pound) pork tenderloin
2 tablespoons olive oil
3 tablespoons brown sugar, divided
1 tablespoon paprika (not smoked)
3¼ teaspoons onion powder, divided
1 teaspoon salt
½ teaspoon white pepper
1 teaspoon garlic powder, divided

½ cup apple juice
½ cup soy sauce
½ cup water
⅓ cup white sugar
2 tablespoons Worcestershire sauce
1½ tablespoons white vinegar
1½ tablespoons vegetable oil
½ teaspoon grated fresh ginger

1. Set Traeger temperature to 225°F and preheat, lid closed for 15 minutes. 2. Trim away any silver skin or hanging pieces of flesh and fat from the tenderloin. Blot dry with paper towels, and brush all over with olive oil. 3. In a small bowl, combine 2 tablespoons brown sugar, paprika, 2 teaspoons onion powder, salt, white pepper, and ½ teaspoon garlic powder. Season the tenderloin on all sides with the rub. 4. Place the tenderloin on the grill grate and cook for 1 hour. After an hour, pour the apple juice into a clean spray bottle and lightly spritz the pork with it. 5. In a medium saucepan over medium-high heat, combine the soy sauce, water, white sugar, Worcestershire sauce, remaining 1 tablespoon of brown sugar, distilled white vinegar, vegetable oil, remaining 1¼ teaspoons of onion powder, remaining ½ teaspoon of garlic powder, and ginger to make the teriyaki glaze. Simmer for 1 minute, stirring often. Reduce heat to medium-low and let the sauce simmer for an additional 4 to 5 minutes. The sauce should reduce down to a syrup-like consistency, able to coat the back of a spoon. Remove from heat, cover, and keep warm. 6. Once the pork reaches an internal temperature of 130°F, it's time to apply the teriyaki glaze. Brush the tenderloin with it every 10 minutes until the internal temperature of the pork reaches 145°F. 7. Remove from the grill and place onto a cutting board. Rest the tenderloin for 10 minutes, then slice and serve.

Flavorful Roasted Suckling Pig

Prep Time: 20 minutes | Cook Time: 4 hours | Serves: 12

1 cup olive oil
Juice of 3 lemons
½ cup tamari
¼ cup dry sherry
¼ cup firmly packed light brown sugar
3 cloves garlic, chopped
2 tablespoons chopped fresh thyme
2 tablespoons chopped fresh flat-leaf parsley

1 teaspoon crushed fennel seeds
Freshly ground black pepper
1 (15-pound) suckling pig, cleaned and dressed (have the butcher do this for you)
Wooden skewers soaked in water for an hour
2 oranges
2 maraschino cherries

1. In a large bowl, whisk the oil, lemon juice, tamari, sherry, brown sugar, garlic, thyme, parsley, and fennel seeds together. Season generously with pepper and whisk again. 2. Using your hands, rub the pig with the marinade, inside and out, working it into the meat. Transfer the pig to a large plastic bag (such as a garbage bag), pour any remaining marinade over the pig, and seal the bag. Put this bag inside another bag and fold closed. Refrigerate for at least 8 hours or overnight. Let the pig come to room temperature in the marinade at least 2 hours but not more than 3 hours before cooking. 3. Set Traeger temperature to 200°F and preheat, lid closed for 15 minutes. 4. Wrap the pig's tail, feet, ears, and snout with aluminum foil to prevent burning. Put an orange in the pig's mouth to hold it open during cooking. Skewer the hind legs into a forward position under the pig. Place the pig in a kneeling position on the grill. Pierce the skin behind the neck several times to prevent the skin from cracking. Close the lid and smoke the pig for about 20 minutes per pound, roughly 4 to 5 hours, until an instant-read thermometer reads 165° F when tested in the rump. After 1 hour, begin basting the pig hourly with the pan drippings, closing the lid after each baste. When close to the end of the cooking time, remove all the foil from the pig. 5. Transfer the pig to a cutting board and let it rest for at least 30 minutes before serving. Replace the orange with a fresh one and put the cherries in the eye cavities, securing them with toothpicks. Remove the skewers from the hind legs. Carve from back to front. When you have cut as much meat as possible this way, tear the rib cage apart into ribs and slice what meat there is from the ribs. Serve immediately.

BBQ Pulled Pork

Prep Time: 15 minutes | Cook Time: 10 hours | Serves: 12

1 bone-in pork shoulder (5 to 7 pounds)
¾ cup apple cider
½ cup granulated sugar
¼ cup kosher salt, plus more for seasoning and sprinkling
¼ cup warm water
2 tablespoons Worcestershire sauce

1 tablespoon hot pepper sauce
Freshly ground black pepper
Lexington-Style "Dip" for serving
Coleslaw for serving
10 to 12 cheap hamburger buns

1. At least 1 hour before you plan to cook, remove the pork from the refrigerator. Combine the cider, sugar, salt, water, Worcestershire, and hot pepper sauce in a jar, close, and shake vigorously until the sugar and salt have dissolved. Load a flavor injector with the cider mixture and inject it into the pork in several places. As you inject and push on the plunger, pull the injector toward you so that the cider mixture doesn't pool in just one place. Season the pork on all sides with salt and pepper. 2. Set Traeger temperature to 200°F and preheat, lid closed for 15 minutes. 3. Place the pork on the grill, close the lid, and smoke for about 6 hours. 4. Working quickly, remove the pork from the grill and double wrap it in aluminum foil. Place it back on the grill, close the lid, and cook for another 4 hours, maintaining the temperature between 200° and 250° F. The pork is ready when you can easily slide out the bone with a pair of tongs. 5. Move the pork to a cutting board and let it cool for about 30 minutes. Using tongs, remove the fat cap and discard. With the tongs and a fork, pull and shred all the meat. Sprinkle with a little additional salt and about ½ cup of the Lexington-Style "Dip". Toss to blend. Pile on a platter and serve with slaw, buns, and additional dip, letting diners make their own pulled-pork sandwiches.

Citrus Pork Butt

Prep Time: 20 minutes | Cook Time: 6 hours | Serves: 12

1 (7-pound) bone-in pork butt
½ cup fresh orange juice
⅓ cup fresh lime juice
¼ cup red wine vinegar
3 tablespoons olive oil
¼ cup chopped fresh flat-leaf parsley
1 tablespoon chopped fresh oregano

1 tablespoon chopped fresh thyme
1 teaspoon ground cumin
2 teaspoons grated orange zest
1 teaspoon grated lime zest
6 cloves garlic, finely minced
½ teaspoon kosher salt
½ teaspoon freshly ground black pepper

1. Lightly score any fat or skin on the pork butt. Place in a 2½-gallon zip-top plastic bag. 2. In a small bowl, whisk the citrus juices, vinegar, oil, herbs, cumin, zest, garlic, salt, and pepper together. Pour the marinade over the pork. Seal and refrigerate for at least 12 hours (24 hours is better). Turn the bag occasionally. Remove from the refrigerator 45 minutes before cooking. 3. Set Traeger temperature to 200°F and preheat, lid closed for 15 minutes. 4. Remove the pork from the marinade and pat dry. Reserve the marinade. Place the pork on the grill, close the lid, and smoke, basting occasionally (no more than once an hour) with the marinade, for about 6 hours, until the bone can easily be pulled out with a pair of tongs and the internal temperature is 190° F. Stop basting during the last 10 to 15 minutes of cooking. 5. Transfer the pork to a cutting board and let rest for 15 minutes. Pull off the skin and as much fat as possible and either slice across the grain or pull apart with two forks.

Juicy Pork Chops

Prep Time: 15 minutes | Cook Time: 2 hours | Serves: 4

1 cup pineapple juice
¼ cup soy sauce
4 garlic cloves, minced
2 tablespoons vegetable oil
2 tablespoons brown sugar
2 teaspoons grated fresh ginger

1 teaspoon Worcestershire sauce
1 teaspoon paprika
½ teaspoon white pepper
2 double-cut pork chops
Pinch salt
Pinch freshly ground black pepper

1. In a medium bowl, combine the pineapple juice, soy sauce, garlic, vegetable oil, brown sugar, ginger, Worcestershire sauce, paprika, and white pepper. 2. Place the pork chops in a large resealable plastic bag, pour in the marinade, and turn the chops to coat evenly, massaging them through the bag. Seal the bag and refrigerate for 4 to 6 hours. 3. Set Traeger temperature to 250°F and preheat, lid closed for 15 minutes. 4. Remove the pork chops from the marinade and lightly shake off any excess marinade. Season with the salt and black pepper. 5. Place the chops directly onto the grill grate, close the lid, and cook for up to 2 hours, or until the internal temperature reaches 140°F. 6. Remove the pork chops and rest them for 10 minutes before serving.

Chapter 6 Lamb and Venison Recipes

74   Venison Steaks with Blackberry Sauce

74   Rosemary-Garlic Rack of Lamb

74   Lamb and Cherry Tomato Kebabs

75   Sweet and Spicy Lamb Ribs

75   Herbed Ground Lamb Kebabs

75   Rosemary-Garlic Leg of Lamb

76   Lemon-Oregano Boneless Leg of Lamb

76   Savory Hoisin-Soy Lamb Shanks

76   Feta Lamb Burgers

77   Aromatic Braised Lamb

77   Herb-Mustard Leg of Lamb

78   Smoked Leg of Lamb with Fresh Mint
      Sauce

78   Lamb Cheeseburgers

78   Barbecued Rack of Lambs

79   Herb-Garlic Rack of Lamb

79   Lamb Chops with Hot Pepper Jelly

79   Dijon Thyme Grilled Rack of Lamb

80   Aromatic Leg of Lamb with Roasted
      Potatoes

80   Herb-Garlic Leg of Lamb with Zucchini
      Salad

81   Basil Marinated Lamb Rib Chops

81   Herb-Butter Crusted Rack of Lamb

81   Curried Lamb Chops with Garlic-
      Yogurt Sauce

82   Juicy Venison Loin Roast

82   Rack of Lamb with Mint Sauce

82   Cumin Lamb Kebabs

Venison Steaks with Blackberry Sauce

Prep Time: 20 minutes | Cook Time: 1 hour | Serves: 4

4 (7- to 8-ounce) venison steaks
1½ tablespoons vegetable oil
1¼ teaspoons kosher salt, plus ⅛ teaspoon
1⅛ teaspoons freshly ground black pepper, divided
1 teaspoon ancho chile powder
5 tablespoons unsalted butter, divided

1 medium shallot, minced
2 cups fresh blackberries, plus more for garnish
½ teaspoon balsamic vinegar
1 cup port wine
1 cup vegetable stock
⅛ teaspoon allspice

1. Set Traeger temperature to 225°F and preheat, lid closed for 15 minutes. 2. Brush the steaks on both sides with vegetable oil. In a small bowl, combine 1¼ teaspoons of salt, 1 teaspoon of black pepper, and the chile powder and rub the mixture into both sides of the steaks. 3. Place the steaks into the grill grate, close the lid, and cook for 1 to 1½ hours, or until the internal temperature reaches 140°F to 145°F. 4. Meanwhile, melt 3 tablespoons of butter in a medium skillet over medium heat, then add the shallot and cook for 2 minutes. Add the blackberries, balsamic vinegar, and port wine, then increase the heat to high and bring the mixture to a boil. Once boiling, reduce the heat to medium-high and simmer until the liquid has reduced by 70 percent. Add the vegetable stock, allspice, remaining ⅛ teaspoon of salt, and remaining ⅛ teaspoon of pepper, and continue simmering until sauce has thickened to a syrup-like consistency. Add the remaining 2 tablespoons of butter and stir through. 5. Strain the sauce through a sieve to remove the blackberry seeds. Return to the pan, cover, and keep warm. 6. Once the venison steaks are done, remove them from the smoker and let rest for 10 minutes. Top with the sauce, garnish with a few fresh blackberries, and serve.

Rosemary-Garlic Rack of Lamb

Prep Time: 25 minutes | Cook Time: 4 hours | Serves: 8

1 (2-pound) rack of lamb

1 batch Rosemary-Garlic Lamb Seasoning

1. Set Traeger temperature to 225°F and preheat, lid closed for 15 minutes. 2. Using a boning knife, score the bottom fat portion of the rib meat. 3. Using your hands, rub the rack of lamb all over with the seasoning, making sure it penetrates into the scored fat. 4. Place the rack directly on the grill grate, fat-side up, and smoke until its internal temperature reaches 145°F. 5. Remove the rack from the grill and let it rest for 20 to 30 minutes, before slicing it into individual ribs to serve.

Lamb and Cherry Tomato Kebabs

Prep Time: 15 minutes | Cook Time: 15 minutes | Serves: 6

1 (2-pound) leg of lamb, cut into 1-inch cubes
½ white onion, cut into 1-inch pieces
1 green bell pepper, cut into 1-inch pieces
1 red bell pepper, cut into 1-inch pieces

½ pound cherry tomatoes
Kosher salt
Freshly ground black pepper

1. If using wooden skewers, soak them in water for 30 to 60 minutes. 2. Set Traeger temperature to 400°F and preheat, lid closed for 15 minutes. 3. Prepare the kebabs, making sure to leave 2 to 3 inches at either end: Thread the skewers alternating lamb, onion, lamb, green bell pepper, lamb, red bell pepper, lamb, cherry tomato, lamb, leaving a small gap between each ingredient. 4. Season the kebabs with salt and pepper to taste. 5. Place the kebabs on the grill grate, close the lid, and cook for about 15 minutes, or until the internal temperature of the meat reaches at least 140°F. 6. Remove the kebabs from the grill and serve immediately.

Sweet and Spicy Lamb Ribs

Prep Time: 15 minutes | Cook Time: 2 hours | Serves: 6

4 racks lamb spareribs (3 to 4 pounds total)
Salt
Freshly ground black pepper

Smoked paprika (optional)
1 (12-ounce) jar grape jelly
½ cup Worcestershire sauce

1. Sprinkle the lamb ribs evenly and liberally on both sides with salt, pepper, and paprika if using. Place them in a shallow pan, cover with plastic wrap, and refrigerate overnight. 2. Remove the ribs from the refrigerator and let stand at room temperature for at least 30 minutes before cooking. 3. Set Traeger temperature to 350°F and preheat, lid closed for 15 minutes. 4. Place the ribs, meaty side down, on the grill. Close the lid and cook for about 10 minutes per side. Remove from the grill and wrap loosely in aluminum foil. Return to the grill and roast for 1½ hours. 5. When the ribs are close to being done, combine the jelly and Worcestershire in a small saucepan over medium heat. Slowly bring to a simmer, whisking, then cook until slightly reduced, about 5 minutes. 6. Remove the ribs from the grill and place in a disposable aluminum-foil pan. Pour the sauce over the ribs and cover tightly with foil. Set the pan on the grill, close the lid, and cook until they are extremely tender, about another 20 minutes. 7. Remove the pan from the grill and place the ribs on a platter. Pour the sauce into a separate bowl and pass at the table.

Herbed Ground Lamb Kebabs

Prep Time: 30 minutes | Cook Time: 8 minutes | Serves: 4

2 pounds ground lamb
2 garlic cloves, finely chopped
2 tablespoons finely chopped fresh parsley
1 tablespoon finely chopped fresh dill
1 tablespoon finely chopped fresh mint
1 tablespoon finely chopped fresh cilantro

1 teaspoon ground coriander
1 teaspoon ground cumin
1 teaspoon paprika
1 teaspoon salt
½ teaspoon black pepper
½ teaspoon ground cinnamon

1. In a large bowl, combine the lamb, garlic, parsley, dill, mint, cilantro, coriander, cumin, paprika, salt, pepper, and cinnamon. Using clean hands, mix until just combined. Do not overmix. 2. Evenly divide the mixture into 8 portions on a cutting board and press each into a rectangle about 4 inches long and 2 inches thick. Lay a metal skewer lengthwise in the center of the rectangles and use your hands to wrap the meat around the skewers, forming a cylinder. Refrigerate for 30 minutes. 3. Set Traeger temperature to 450°F and preheat, lid closed for 15 minutes. 4. Place the lamb kebabs on the grill, uncovered, for 8 to 10 minutes, turning every 2 to 3 minutes, until the internal temperature reaches 160°F. 5. Let the meat rest for 5 minutes, then serve as desired.

Rosemary-Garlic Leg of Lamb

Prep Time: 15 minutes | Cook Time: 5 hours | Serves: 10

1 (6- to 8-pound) boneless leg of lamb
2 tablespoons olive oil

Rosemary-Garlic Seasoning

1. Set Traeger temperature to 180°F and preheat, lid closed for 15 minutes. 2. Rub the lamb with the olive oil and then rub with a generous amount of the seasoning, rubbing underneath and around any netting. 3. Place the lamb directly on the grill grate and close the lid. 4. Smoke at 180°F for 4 to 6 hours, or until the internal temperature reaches 130°F. 5. Increase the temperature to 400°F and continue smoking for 45 minutes to 1 hour, or until the internal temperature reaches 145°F. 6. Remove the lamb from the grill and let rest for 20 to 30 minutes. 7. Remove any netting, slice, and serve.

Lemon-Oregano Boneless Leg of Lamb

Prep Time: 25 minutes | Cook Time: 3 hours | Serves: 8

Zest and juice of 2 lemons
2 tablespoons olive oil
4 garlic cloves, minced
1 medium shallot, minced
¼ cup finely chopped fresh oregano

2 teaspoons finely chopped fresh thyme
2 teaspoons salt
1½ teaspoons freshly ground black pepper
1 (4-pound) boneless leg of lamb

1. In a nonreactive bowl, combine the lemon zest, lemon juice, olive oil, garlic, shallot, oregano, thyme, salt, and black pepper. Set aside. 2. Remove any large clumps of fat and silver skin from the surface of the lamb. Pat the entire leg dry. Unroll the lamb leg to expose the inner portion. Brush with some of the lemon-oregano mixture, then turn it over and brush the rest of the mixture on the outer part. Reroll the lamb and place into a glass baking dish. Cover tightly with plastic wrap and marinate in the refrigerator for 4 hours. 3. Remove the lamb leg from the refrigerator, uncover, and secure the roll with kitchen twine. Let stand at room temperature for 30 minutes. 4. Set Traeger temperature to 250°F and preheat, lid closed for 15 minutes. 5. Place the lamb on the grill grate, close the lid, and cook for 2½ to 3 hours, or until the lamb reaches an internal temperature of between 135°F and 140°F (medium-rare to medium). 6. Remove the lamb from the grill, tent with aluminum foil, and let rest for 10 minutes. Remove the twine, cut the lamb into ½-inch-thick slices, and serve.

Savory Hoisin-Soy Lamb Shanks

Prep Time: 25 minutes | Cook Time: 4 hours | Serves: 4

2 (2-pound) lamb shanks
½ teaspoon salt
½ teaspoon freshly ground black pepper
¾ cup hoisin sauce
¾ cup beef broth
¼ cup freshly squeezed orange juice
2 tablespoons brown sugar

1 teaspoon freshly squeezed lemon juice
2 garlic cloves, minced
2 teaspoons grated ginger
1 tablespoon tomato paste
¼ teaspoon white pepper
¼ teaspoon cinnamon
¼ teaspoon red pepper flakes

1. Set Traeger temperature to 250°F and preheat, lid closed for 15 minutes. 2. Blot the lamb shanks with paper towels. Using a sharp knife, remove the silver skin around the shank and season with the salt and pepper. 3. Place the shanks into the grill, close the lid, and cook for 1½ to 2 hours, or until they reach an internal temperature of 165°F. Remove and place onto a cutting board. 4. Increase the heat of the grill to 325°F. 5. Combine the hoisin sauce, beef broth, orange juice, brown sugar, lemon juice, garlic, ginger, tomato paste, white pepper, cinnamon, and red pepper flakes in a medium bowl. 6. Place the shanks in a 9-inch-by-9-inch disposable aluminum pan. Pour the braising liquid over them and then place the pan back into the grill, uncovered, for 45 minutes. Add more beef broth if needed. 7. Cover the pan with aluminum foil (or place a lid on the pot) and cook for an additional 1½ to 2 hours, or until the lamb reaches an internal temperature of 200°F to 205°F. 8. Remove the lamb shanks from the grill and uncover. Let stand for 10 to 15 minutes. 9. Shred the meat and place it back into the braising liquid, mixing to combine. Serve with your favorite side dish or in tacos with sliced chile peppers and pickled vegetables.

Feta Lamb Burgers

Prep Time: 20 minutes | Cook Time: 10 minutes | Serves: 4

2 pounds ground lamb
4 teaspoons kosher salt
Freshly ground black pepper
4 kaiser rolls, split

1 cup tzatziki
Sliced red onion, for topping
½ cup crumbled feta cheese, for topping

1. Set Traeger temperature to 500°F and preheat, lid closed for 15 minutes. 2. Meanwhile, in a large bowl, combine the lamb with the salt and pepper. Using your hands, mix until just incorporated; form into four 1-inch-thick patties with a slight dimple in the center. 3. Put the burgers on the grill grate. Close the lid and cook, flipping halfway through, for 8 to 10 minutes total for medium, or until an instant-read thermometer inserted into the center registers 135°F. (If using store-bought ground lamb, always cook it to 160°F, or well done.) In the last minute of cooking, place the rolls cut-side down on the grate to toast. 4. Spread the tzatziki on the buns and assemble the burgers, topping them with the onion and feta. Serve immediately.

Aromatic Braised Lamb

Prep Time: 15 minutes | Cook Time: 1½ hours | Serves: 6

2 pounds bone-in lamb shanks
Kosher salt
1 tablespoon ghee or unsalted butter
1 medium red onion, coarsely chopped
4 garlic cloves, finely chopped
1 (1-inch) piece fresh ginger, peeled and finely chopped
2 tablespoons tomato paste
4 bay leaves

2 teaspoons ground coriander
1½ teaspoons ground cardamom
1 teaspoon ground cinnamon
1 teaspoon ground turmeric
10 cloves
5 dried red chiles, such as chile de árbol
2¾ cups water
½ cup Greek yogurt

1. Season the lamb generously with salt. Refrigerate overnight. 2. Pat the lamb dry. 3. Set Traeger temperature to 500°F, then preheat a 5-quart cast iron Dutch oven on the grate with the grill lid closed. 4. Put the ghee in the Dutch oven and close the grill lid. Once hot, add the lamb in a single layer. Close the grill lid and cook, turning halfway through, for 10 to 12 minutes total or until browned on both sides. Transfer to a plate. 5. Add the onion to the Dutch oven. Close the grill lid and cook, stirring occasionally, for 2 to 3 minutes or until starting to soften. Season with salt. 6. Add the garlic and ginger. Close the grill lid and cook, stirring frequently, for 30 to 60 seconds or until fragrant. 7. Add the tomato paste, bay leaves, coriander, cardamom, cinnamon, turmeric, cloves, and chiles and stir to combine. Cook, stirring, for 1 to 2 minutes or until the tomato paste turns bright red. Season with salt. 8. Add the lamb; turn to coat with the tomato-spice mixture. Add the water. Cover the Dutch oven with a tight-fitting lid. Remove from the heat. 9. Wearing barbecue gloves, carefully remove the grate, install the heat deflector, and replace the grate. Reduce the grill temperature to 350°F. 10. Put the Dutch oven back on the grate. Close the grill lid and cook for 55 minutes to 1 hour 5 minutes or until the lamb is tender. 11. Stir in the yogurt. Cook for 5 minutes or until the flavors meld. Serve immediately.

Herb-Mustard Leg of Lamb

Prep Time: 15 minutes | Cook Time: 1½ hours | Serves: 8

1 (4- to 5-pound) boneless or 1 (6- to 8-pound) bone-in leg of lamb
¾ cup vegetable oil
½ cup red wine vinegar
½ cup chopped onion
2 cloves garlic, bruised

2 teaspoons Dijon mustard
2 teaspoons kosher salt
½ teaspoon dried oregano
½ teaspoon dried basil
1 bay leaf
⅛ teaspoon freshly ground black pepper

1. If working with a bone-in leg, have your butcher bone the leg and butterfly it. Place the lamb in a 2½-gallon zip-top plastic bag. 2. In a medium bowl, whisk the oil, vinegar, onion, garlic, mustard, salt, oregano, basil, bay leaf, and pepper together. Add to the bag, seal, and squish the marinade all around to coat the lamb. Refrigerate for 48 hours, turning the bag over occasionally. 3. Remove the lamb from the marinade, reserving the marinade. Pat the lamb dry and let sit at room temperature for about 30 minutes. Bring the marinade to a full boil in a small saucepan over high heat. Reduce the heat slightly and cook for 5 minutes. Remove from the heat and let cool. 4. Set Traeger temperature to 500°F and preheat, lid closed for 15 minutes. 5. Set the lamb on the grill, close the lid, and sear about 5 minutes per side. Remove the lamb from the grill. 6. Set the lamb on a rack in a roasting pan and put the pan on the grill. Close the lid and adjust the grill temperature to 350° F. Roast until the internal temperature at the thickest point of the lamb registers 135° F, about 1 to 1½ hours. 7. Transfer the lamb to a cutting board and let rest for 10 minutes. The lamb will be crusty on the outside and cooked to multiple levels of doneness, from rare to well done. Cut into slices and serve with the reserved marinade, reheated, as a dipping sauce.

Smoked Leg of Lamb with Fresh Mint Sauce

Prep Time: 20 minutes | Cook Time: 5 hours | Serves: 8

For the Mint Sauce:
½ cup apple cider vinegar
¼ cup water
¼ cup sugar

1 teaspoon salt
½ cup fresh mint leaves, finely chopped

For the Lamb:
½ cup olive oil
½ cup white wine
½ cup apple cider vinegar
1 tablespoon minced garlic

2 teaspoons salt
2 teaspoons freshly ground black pepper
1 (5-pound) leg of lamb

To make the mint sauce: 1. In a small saucepan on the stovetop over medium heat, whisk together the vinegar, water, sugar, and salt. Bring the mixture to a boil. Reduce the heat and simmer for 5 minutes, uncovered. 2. Remove the sauce from the heat, and stir in the mint leaves. Let the sauce cool and refrigerate it until ready to serve.

To make the lamb: 1. In a medium bowl, whisk together the olive oil, wine, vinegar, garlic, salt, and pepper to make a marinade. 2. Place the leg of lamb in a shallow dish, and pour the marinade over it. 3. Cover the dish with plastic wrap, and refrigerate for 4 hours. 4. Set Traeger temperature to 225°F and preheat, lid closed for 15 minutes. 5. Remove the lamb from the refrigerator, and discard the marinade. Do not rinse. 6. Place the lamb on the grill grate and smoke for 4 to 5 hours, until the internal temperature registers 135°F. 7. Remove the lamb from the heat. Let rest for 15 to 20 minutes. The temperature will increase about 5°F, bringing the final internal temperature to 140°F for serving. 8. Serve the lamb with the mint sauce.

Lamb Cheeseburgers

Prep Time: 10 minutes | Cook Time: 12 minutes | Serves: 6

2 pounds ground lamb, preferably from the shoulder or leg
1 cup finely chopped fresh white mushrooms
1 tablespoon finely minced garlic
2 teaspoons finely minced fresh rosemary
1 tablespoon kosher salt

1 tablespoon coarsely ground black pepper
6 slices fontina cheese
3 tablespoons unsalted butter, at room temperature
6 whole-wheat buns or whole-wheat pita breads
Tzatziki Sauce, optional

1. In a large bowl, using a light hand, gently work the lamb, mushrooms, garlic, rosemary, salt, and pepper together. Divide the mixture into 6 equal portions and gently form into 1-inch-thick patties. Take your thumb and make a good ¼-inch depression in the middle of each patty; this will keep them from puffing up on the grill. Refrigerate until ready to cook. 2. Set Traeger temperature to 500°F and preheat, lid closed for 15 minutes. 3. Place the patties on the grill, close the lid, and cook to your desired doneness. That should be 5 to 7 minutes per side, or an internal temperature of 140°F. When you turn the burgers, place a slice of cheese on top of each. With about 2 minutes left in the cooking time, butter the buns and place them, cut side down, on the grill to toast. 4. When done, transfer the burgers and buns to a warm platter. Place a burger on the bottom half of each bun and top with the tzatziki.

Barbecued Rack of Lambs

Prep Time: 15 minutes | Cook Time: 12 minutes | Serves: 2

2 tablespoons paprika
2 teaspoons salt
½ teaspoon garlic powder
½ teaspoon onion powder

½ teaspoon black pepper
1 small (1½-pound) whole rack of lamb, cut into individual chops
Juice of 2 lemons

1. In a small bowl, stir together the paprika, salt, garlic powder, onion powder, and pepper until thoroughly combined. Coat each lamb chop with lemon juice, then coat the entire chop with the seasoning mix. 2. Put the seasoned lamb chops in a large bowl, cover, and refrigerate to marinate for 1 to 3 hours. 3. Set Traeger temperature to 480°F and preheat, lid closed for 15 minutes. 4. Place the chops on the grill. Close the lid and grill for 5 to 6 minutes per side until the chops reach an internal temperature of 145°F. 5. Rest. Let the chops rest for 5 minutes, then serve immediately.

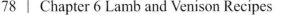

Herb-Garlic Rack of Lamb

Prep Time: 1 hour | Cook Time: 1½ hours | Serves: 4

2 racks of lamb, trimmed, frenched, and tied into a crown
1¼ cups extra-virgin olive oil, divided
2 tablespoons chopped fresh basil
2 tablespoons chopped fresh rosemary
2 tablespoons ground sage

2 tablespoons ground thyme
8 garlic cloves, minced
2 teaspoons salt
2 teaspoons freshly ground black pepper

1. Set the lamb out on the counter to take the chill off, about an hour. 2. In a small bowl, combine 1 cup of olive oil, the basil, rosemary, sage, thyme, garlic, salt, and pepper. 3. Baste the entire crown with the herbed olive oil and wrap the exposed frenched bones in aluminum foil. 4. Set Traeger temperature to 275°F and preheat, lid closed for 15 minutes. 5. Put the lamb directly on the grill, close the lid, and smoke for 1 hour 30 minutes to 2 hours, or until a meat thermometer inserted in the thickest part reads 140°F. 6. Remove the lamb from the heat, tent with foil, and let rest for about 15 minutes before serving. The temperature will rise about 5°F during the rest period, for a finished temperature of 145°F.

Lamb Chops with Hot Pepper Jelly

Prep Time: 15 minutes | Cook Time: 20 minutes | Serves: 4

For the Marinade:
½ cup rice wine vinegar
1 teaspoon liquid smoke
2 tablespoons extra-virgin olive oil
For the Lamb Chops:
8 (4-ounce) lamb chops
½ cup hot pepper jelly
1 tablespoon Sriracha

2 tablespoons dried minced onion
1 tablespoon chopped fresh mint

1 teaspoon salt
1 teaspoon freshly ground black pepper

To make the marinade: In a small bowl, whisk together the rice wine vinegar, liquid smoke, olive oil, minced onion, and mint.
To make the lamb chops: 1. Place the lamb chops in an aluminum roasting pan. Pour the marinade over the meat, turning to coat thoroughly. Cover with plastic wrap and marinate in the refrigerator for 2 hours. 2. Set Traeger temperature to 165°F and preheat, lid closed for 15 minutes. 3. On the stove top, in a small saucepan over low heat, combine the hot pepper jelly and Sriracha and keep warm. 4. When ready to cook the chops, remove them from the marinade and pat dry. Discard the marinade. 5. Season the chops with the salt and pepper, then place them directly on the grill grate, close the lid, and smoke for 5 minutes. 6. Increase the temperature to 450°F. Once the grill is up to temperature, sear the chops 2 minutes per side to achieve medium-rare chops. A meat thermometer inserted in the thickest part of the meat should read 145°F. Continue grilling, if necessary, to your desired doneness. 7. Serve the chops with the warm Sriracha pepper jelly on the side.

Dijon Thyme Grilled Rack of Lamb

Prep Time: 15 minutes | Cook Time: 40 minutes | Serves: 4

⅓ cup Dijon mustard
2 tablespoons ketchup
1 tablespoon Worcestershire sauce
1 tablespoon fresh lemon juice

¼ cup chopped fresh thyme or lemon thyme (preferred)
2 (1½-pound) racks of lamb, Frenched if desired
¼ cup olive oil

1. In a small bowl, whisk the mustard, ketchup, Worcestershire, lemon juice, and thyme together, then brush the mixture liberally over the lamb. Cover with plastic wrap and refrigerate overnight. Reserve the remaining marinade. 2. Wipe the marinade off the lamb, then brush the lamb with the olive oil. 3. Set Traeger temperature to 500°F and preheat, lid closed for 15 minutes. 4. Place the lamb on the grill and sear for a couple of minutes on each side. Remove the lamb from the grill and brush on both sides with the reserved marinade. 5. Set the lamb racks in a roasting pan and set the pan on the grill. Close the lid and roast until the internal temperature reads 125°F, 20 to 30 minutes, brushing with the marinade again halfway through. 6. Transfer the racks to a cutting board and let rest at least 10 minutes before cutting into individual or double chops. Serve at once.

Aromatic Leg of Lamb with Roasted Potatoes

Prep Time: 20 minutes | Cook Time: 2½ to 3 hours | Serves: 8

4 cloves garlic, minced
¼ cup fresh rosemary leaves
¼ cup fresh oregano leaves
¼ cup fresh mint leaves
2 tablespoons sugar
2 tablespoons coriander seeds
1 tablespoon red pepper flakes
Kosher salt and freshly ground black pepper

1 (6-pound) leg of lamb
4 pounds medium Yukon Gold potatoes, sliced ½ inch thick
1 large lemons, sliced ½ inch thick
1 head garlic, split in half
4 small sprigs fresh rosemary
Olive oil
Mint jelly for serving (optional)

1. The day before you intend to cook the lamb, combine the minced garlic, rosemary, oregano, and mint leaves, sugar, coriander, red pepper flakes, and a good amount of salt and black pepper in a food processor and pulse until it forms a paste. Score the fat around the leg in a crisscross pattern to allow the paste to penetrate the meat. Rub all of the paste into the leg. Wrap the leg tightly with plastic wrap and refrigerate overnight. 2. Remove the lamb from the refrigerator, rinse the paste off, pat dry, and let the chill come off of it for about 1 hour. Season the lamb with salt and black pepper. 3. In the meantime, arrange the potato slices in layers in a large cast-iron skillet or sheet pan in as even a layer as you can get. Place the lemon slices on top along with the split head of garlic and rosemary sprigs. Season generously with salt and black pepper and give it a drizzle of olive oil. 4. Set Traeger temperature to 200°F and preheat, lid closed for 15 minutes. 5. Place the pan of potatoes on the grill grate and position the lamb directly above the potatoes. Close the lid and smoke for 2½ to 3 hours, letting the juices from the meat drip down onto the potatoes, until the internal temperature of the lamb at the thickest point reaches 140° F. 6. Transfer the lamb to a cutting board, tent with aluminum foil, and let it rest for at least 20 minutes. Check the doneness of the potatoes and, if needed, let them continue to cook. Slice the lamb thinly and serve with the potatoes and a lemon slice and mint jelly if desired.

Herb-Garlic Leg of Lamb with Zucchini Salad

Prep Time: 35 minutes | Cook Time: 30 minutes | Serves: 8

Marinade:
¼ cup extra-virgin olive oil
1 tablespoon finely chopped fresh rosemary leaves
1 tablespoon minced garlic
1 teaspoon kosher salt
Salad:
12 ounces small zucchini, trimmed and halved lengthwise
1 small red onion, cut into ½-inch-thick slices
Extra-virgin olive oil
8 ounces cherry tomatoes, cut into halves
2 tablespoons pitted, chopped Kalamata olives

½ teaspoon coarse-ground black pepper
1 boneless leg of lamb, 3 to 4 pounds, butterflied, trimmed of fat, and cut into 3 or 4 equal sections

2 tablespoons drained, finely chopped oil-packed sun-dried tomatoes
2 tablespoons finely chopped fresh mint leaves
Lemon-Parsley Dressing

1. In a small bowl, whisk together all the marinade ingredients. Place the lamb in a large, resealable plastic bag and pour in the marinade. Press the air out of the bag and seal tightly. Turn the bag to distribute the marinade evenly, place the bag in a bowl, and refrigerate for 2 to 12 hours, turning the bag occasionally. 2. Set Traeger temperature to 400°F and preheat, lid closed for 15 minutes. 3. Brush the zucchini and onion evenly with oil. Place them on the grill grate, with the lid closed, until barely tender, 5 to 7 minutes, turning once. Remove from the grill. Let cool slightly, then cut the zucchini on the diagonal into ½-inch-thick slices and chop the onion. In a serving bowl combine the zucchini, onion, cherry tomatoes, olives, sun-dried tomatoes, and mint. 4. Spoon 3 tablespoons of the dressing over the salad. Toss to coat evenly. Reserve the remaining dressing. 5. Meanwhile, place the lamb pieces on the other side of the grill grate, with the lid closed, until cooked to your desired doneness, turning once. Pieces more than 2 inches thick will take 20 to 30 minutes to reach medium rare (145°F); pieces 1 to 2 inches thick will take 15 to 20 minutes. Remove the lamb from the grill and let rest for 5 minutes. 6. Cut the lamb across the grain into thin slices. Spoon the reserved dressing over the meat. Serve warm with the salad.

Basil Marinated Lamb Rib Chops

Prep Time: 15 minutes | Cook Time: 10 minutes | Serves: 6

3 tablespoons stone-ground mustard
1 large clove garlic, peeled
2 tablespoons balsamic vinegar
½ teaspoon kosher salt
Freshly ground black pepper

½ cup extra-virgin olive oil
¼ cup slivered fresh basil
16 rib lamb chops, trimmed of excess fat (this is two half racks of lamb, about 4 pounds total)
Chopped fresh flat-leaf parsley for garnish

1. Place the mustard, garlic, vinegar, salt, and black pepper to taste in a blender and pulse to combine. With the machine running, slowly pour in the olive oil. Pour the mixture into a small bowl and stir in the basil. 2. Place the chops in a 2½-gallon zip-top plastic bag. Add the marinade and squish around to evenly coat the chops. Seal the bag and refrigerate for 4 hours. Remove from the refrigerator at least 30 minutes before cooking. 3. Set Traeger temperature to 500°F and preheat, lid closed for 15 minutes. 4. Remove the chops from the marinade and wipe off any excess. Place the chops on the grill grate, close the lid, and cook until the chops feel like the tip of your nose when pressed, about 5 minutes per side. This will result in a medium-rare chop with an internal temperature of about 130°F. 5. Transfer the chops to a platter and let rest for 5 to10 minutes. Sprinkle with the parsley and serve.

Herb-Butter Crusted Rack of Lamb

Prep Time: 15 minutes | Cook Time: 1½ hours | Serves: 6

2 (2-pound) racks of lamb
¼ cup unsalted butter, softened
3 tablespoons Dijon mustard
2 tablespoons red wine vinegar
4 garlic cloves, minced
2½ teaspoons kosher salt

2 teaspoons Worcestershire sauce
2 teaspoons finely chopped fresh rosemary
2 teaspoons finely chopped fresh thyme
2 teaspoons finely chopped fresh marjoram
½ teaspoon freshly ground black pepper

1. Set Traeger temperature to 225°F and preheat, lid closed for 15 minutes. 2. Remove any large clumps of fat and silver skin from the rack of lamb. 3. In a medium bowl, combine the softened butter, Dijon mustard, red wine vinegar, garlic, salt, Worcestershire sauce, rosemary, thyme, marjoram, and black pepper. Apply this mixture onto the meat of the racks, avoiding the bones. 4. Place the racks into the grill, bone-side down, close the lid, and cook for 1 to 1½ hours, or until the internal temperature of the lamb reaches between 135°F and 145°F (medium to medium-well). 5. Remove from the grill and let rest for 10 minutes before carving.

Curried Lamb Chops with Garlic-Yogurt Sauce

Prep Time: 20 minutes | Cook Time: 10 minutes | Serves: 4

Sauce:
½ cup plain whole-milk Greek yogurt
1 tablespoon finely chopped cilantro leaves
2 teaspoons lime juice
1 teaspoon chile-garlic paste
Marinade:
3 tablespoons lime juice
2 tablespoons peeled, finely grated fresh ginger
2 tablespoons extra-virgin olive oil
2 teaspoons Madras curry powder
1 teaspoon smoked paprika

½ garlic clove, minced
¼ teaspoon kosher salt
⅛ teaspoon garam masala

1 teaspoon ground turmeric
1 teaspoon cayenne pepper
1 teaspoon kosher salt
1 teaspoon freshly ground black pepper
8 lamb loin chops, each 1½ inches thick, trimmed

1. In a small bowl, whisk together all the sauce ingredients. Cover and refrigerate until 30 minutes before serving. (The sauce can be made up to 8 hours in advance.) 2. In a separate small bowl, whisk together all the marinade ingredients. Place the lamb chops in a large glass baking dish, pour the marinade over them, and turn the chops to coat evenly. Cover and refrigerate for at least 2 hours or up to 4 hours. Let the chops stand at room temperature for 15 to 30 minutes before grilling. 3. Set Traeger temperature to 400°F and preheat, lid closed for 15 minutes. 4. Remove the chops from the dish and discard the marinade. Place the chops on the grill grate, with the lid closed, until cooked to your desired doneness, 8 to 10 minutes for medium rare, turning once. Remove from the grill and let rest for 3 to 5 minutes. 5. Serve the chops warm, with the yogurt sauce alongside.

Juicy Venison Loin Roast

Prep Time: 20 minutes | Cook Time: 1½ hours | Serves: 4

1 (1- to 1½-pound) venison loin roast
½ cup pineapple juice
2 tablespoons dark rum
2½ tablespoons soy sauce
1 tablespoon vegetable oil

1½ teaspoons grated fresh ginger
4 garlic cloves, minced
1 to 2 teaspoons chili sauce (such as sambal oelek or sriracha)
¼ teaspoon white pepper
½ teaspoon salt

1. Place the venison loin in a resealable plastic bag. In a medium bowl, combine the pineapple juice, rum, soy sauce, vegetable oil, ginger, garlic, chili sauce, and white pepper. Pour the marinade over the venison and work it into the meat. Seal the bag and place in the refrigerator for 6 to 12 hours. 2. Set Traeger temperature to 225°F and preheat, lid closed for 15 minutes. 3. Remove the loin from the refrigerator and discard the excess marinade. Season the loin with the salt, and place on the grill grate. Close the lid and cook for 1½ to 2 hours, or until the internal temperature is five degrees away from your desired doneness. 4. Promptly remove the loin from the grill and let it rest for 10 minutes. Slice and serve.

Rack of Lamb with Mint Sauce

Prep Time: 20 minutes | Cook Time: 1¼ hours | Serves: 4

For the Paste:
½ cup olive oil
½ cup dry mustard
¼ cup hot chili powder
2 tablespoons freshly squeezed lemon juice
2 tablespoons dry minced onion
1 tablespoon smoked paprika

1 tablespoon dried thyme
1 tablespoon Worcestershire sauce
1 teaspoon salt
1 American rack of lamb (7 or 8 chops), membrane along the back of the rack removed

For the Mint Sauce:
¼ cup fresh mint leaves, chopped
¼ cup hot water
2 tablespoons apple cider vinegar

2 tablespoons firmly packed brown sugar
½ teaspoon salt
½ teaspoon freshly ground black pepper

To make the paste: 1. In a small bowl, whisk together the olive oil, mustard, chili powder, lemon juice, onion, paprika, thyme, Worcestershire sauce, and salt. Set aside. 2. Set Traeger temperature to 200°F and preheat, lid closed for 15 minutes. 3. Rub the paste all over the lamb and place it on the grill grate. Smoke for 1¼ hours until it reaches an internal temperature of 145°F. 4. Remove the lamb from the heat and let it rest for a few minutes before serving with the mint sauce.
To make the mint sauce: While the lamb smokes, in a small bowl, stir together the mint, water, vinegar, brown sugar, salt, and pepper. Set aside until serving.

Cumin Lamb Kebabs

Prep Time: 15 minutes | Cook Time: 8 minutes | Serves: 6

2 tablespoons finely chopped fresh parsley
2 tablespoons finely chopped fresh cilantro
2 scallions, finely chopped
1 teaspoon ground cumin
1 teaspoon paprika

½ teaspoon salt
½ teaspoon white pepper
2 tablespoons olive oil
2 pounds lamb shoulder or leg meat, cut into 1-inch cubes

1. In a large bowl, stir together the parsley, cilantro, scallions, cumin, paprika, salt, white pepper, and olive oil until well mixed. Add the lamb cubes and mix until well coated. Cover and let marinate at room temperature for 1 hour. 2. Skewer the lamb. Thread the marinated lamb onto 8 metal skewers. Set aside while you prepare the grill. 3. Set Traeger temperature to 4750°F and preheat, lid closed for 15 minutes. 4. Oil the cooking grates, then place the kebabs on the grill grate and grill for 8 to 10 minutes, turning every 2 minutes, until the lamb reaches an internal temperature of 145°F. 5. Let the lamb rest for 5 minutes, then serve immediately.

Chapter 7 Fish and Seafood Recipes

84 Grilled Cajun Mahi-Mahi

84 Cedar-Plank Grilled Salmon

84 Cedar Plank Grilled Salmon

85 Delicious Salmon Candy

85 Grilled Oysters with Lemon-Garlic Sauce

85 Spiced Salmon Fillets

86 Spiced Sea Bass

86 Halibut with Tomato-Herb Sauce

86 Savory Crab Cakes with Spicy Mayo

87 Blackened Tilapia Tacos

87 Bacon-Wrapped Scallops with Cilantro Butter

87 Lemon Garlic Lobster Tail Skewers

88 Garlic Butter Crawfish Skewers

88 Maple-Walnut Crusted Salmon

88 Marinated Mahimahi with Bang Bang Sauce

89 Tuna Sliders with Wasabi Broccoli Slaw

89 Seared Scallops and Cheese Grits

90 Shrimp-Zucchini Kabobs with Pistachio-Tarragon Pesto

90 Lemon Cheese Risotto with Grilled Asparagus & Shrimp

91 Crunchy Shrimp and Scallop Skewers

91 Grilled Shrimp, Corn and Avocado Salad

91 Easy Grilled Salmon

92 Grilled Lobster Tails with Tarragon Butter

92 Cheese-Spinach Stuffed Salmon

92 Grilled Salmon with Tarragon

93 Seafood Stew with Garlic Croutons

93 Hearty Shrimp, Chicken, and Sausage Paella

94 BBQ Lemon Trout

94 Teriyaki Shrimp-Pineapple Skewers

Grilled Cajun Mahi-Mahi

Prep Time: 15 minutes | Cook Time: 6 minutes | Serves: 4

1 to 4 (6-ounce) mahi-mahi fillets
1 cup Quick and Easy Goes-with-Everything Marinade

¼ cup Cajun Spice Rub
1 to 6 lemon wedges, for garnish

1. Place the fillets in large zip-top bag (or a bowl with a lid) and cover them with the marinade. Marinate for about 30 minutes in the refrigerator. 2. Set Traeger temperature to 450°F and preheat, lid closed for 15 minutes. 3. Remove the fish from the marinade and blot it with a paper towel. 4. Season both sides of each fillet with a light coating of the Cajun Spice Rub. 5. Oil your cooking grates with a light coating of vegetable oil to help prevent the fish from sticking. 6. Place the fillets on the grill directly and cook for 6 minutes. Flip them every 2 minutes, using a spatula to get those crosshatch grill marks. 7. Remove from the heat and serve with lemon wedges.

Cedar-Plank Grilled Salmon

Prep Time: 1 hour 30 minutes | Cook Time: 15 minutes | Serves: 4

½ cup Cajun Spice Rub
1 tablespoon brown sugar (optional)

2 (1-pound) fresh salmon fillets, skin on
Lemon slices, for garnish

1. Soak 2 cedar grilling planks in fresh water for about 1 hour. You can weigh them down with a plate or something heavy to make sure they're completely submerged. 2. Mix the Cajun Spice Rub with the brown sugar (if using—it's optional but works very well with salmon). 3. Set Traeger temperature to 450°F and preheat, lid closed for 15 minutes. 4. Place the cedar planks on the grill grate, without the fillets on them. You want to get the planks preheated and kill off any pathogens. After you hear a couple pops, flip the planks. You should see a very light toasty char on them. 5. Place the salmon on top of the planks, skin-side down, and close the lid. 6. Check the internal temperature of your fish; 140°F will give you nice medium doneness, and the flesh should be easily flaked with a fork, about 15 minutes. 7. When it's done, scrape the fish off the planks with a sturdy spatula and serve.

Cedar Plank Grilled Salmon

Prep Time: 20 minutes | Cook Time: 1 hour | Serves: 4

4 (6-ounce) salmon fillets
2 tablespoons reduced-sodium soy sauce
2 tablespoons vegetable oil
2 tablespoons balsamic vinegar
1 tablespoon chili sauce
1 tablespoon brown sugar

½ teaspoon sesame oil
2 scallions, chopped, white and green parts separated
2 garlic cloves, minced
1 teaspoon grated fresh ginger
¼ teaspoon salt
1 large untreated cedar plank, or 2 small ones

1. Place the salmon fillets, skin-side down, into a glass baking dish. In a medium bowl, whisk together the soy sauce, vegetable oil, balsamic vinegar, chili sauce, brown sugar, sesame oil, the white parts of the scallions, garlic, ginger, and salt. Pour the sauce evenly over the salmon. Cover the dish with plastic wrap and refrigerate for 1 hour. At the same time, soak the cedar plank in tepid water for 1 hour. 2. Set Traeger temperature to 225°F and preheat, lid closed for 15 minutes. 3. Once preheated, place the presoaked plank on the grate to heat up, about 4 to 5 minutes. Once it becomes aromatic, place the marinated salmon pieces on the plank, skin-side down, close the lid, and cook for 1 hour, or until the internal temperature of the salmon reaches 140°F. Remove from the grill and serve immediately.

Delicious Salmon Candy

Prep Time: 20 minutes | Cook Time: 3 hours | Serves: 8

2¼ cups brown sugar
1½ cups kosher salt

5 pounds skin-on salmon, cut into 1½-inch strips
1¼ cups real maple syrup

1. In a medium bowl, combine the brown sugar and salt. Fill a large glass dish or resealable plastic container ¼ inch deep with the mixture. Place the strips, skin-side down, into the mixture. Spread them out a little, as the salmon will need room to cure. If you need to build another layer, repeat the process with ¼ inch of the curing mixture between the layers. Cover and refrigerate for 2 hours. 2. Remove the fish, rinse it off under cold water, and blot dry with paper towels. Place the strips in a clean dish or pan and let them dry in the refrigerator for 24 hours uncovered. 3. Set Traeger temperature to 165°F and preheat, lid closed for 15 minutes. 4. Place the salmon strips directly onto the grill grate. Gradually bring the temperature up to 200°F. Smoke the fish for 3 to 4 hours total, depending on thickness and desired texture. Every 90 minutes, brush the salmon with the maple syrup. 5. Once cooked, the candied salmon will have a deep color with a shiny finish. Remove from the grill and place onto cooling racks for 1 hour before serving or eating. Store in the refrigerator or freezer in a vacuum-sealed bag.

Grilled Oysters with Lemon-Garlic Sauce

Prep Time: 15 minutes | Cook Time: 8 minutes | Serves: 4

8 tablespoons (1 stick) butter
4 garlic cloves, minced
2 tablespoons freshly squeezed lemon juice

¼ teaspoon salt
¼ teaspoon black pepper
24 fresh oysters, rinsed and cleaned

1. In saucepan over medium heat, melt the butter. Add the garlic and cook for 1 to 2 minutes, until tender. Stir in the lemon juice, salt, and pepper. Simmer the sauce for 3 to 4 minutes, then set aside for serving. 2. Set Traeger temperature to 425°F and preheat, lid closed for 15 minutes. 3. Oil the cooking grates, then place the oysters on the grill grate and close the lid. Cook for 4 to 6 minutes, turning every 2 to 3 minutes, until the oyster shells pop open. Cook for about 2 minutes more once opened, then remove from the grill. 4. Discard any oysters that have not opened. Serve the oysters with the lemon-garlic sauce on the side for dipping.

Spiced Salmon Fillets

Prep Time: 15 minutes | Cook Time: 4 minutes | Serves: 4

¼ cup paprika
2 tablespoons light brown sugar
1 tablespoon salt
1 tablespoon black pepper
1 tablespoon chili powder

1 tablespoon garlic powder
1 tablespoon onion powder
4 (about 1½ pounds total) salmon fillets, skinned
2 tablespoons olive oil

1. In a small bowl, stir together the paprika, brown sugar, salt, pepper, chili powder, garlic powder, and onion powder until blended. Brush each salmon fillet with olive oil. Sprinkle a generous amount of barbecue rub on each side of the salmon fillets. 2. Set Traeger temperature to 425°F and preheat, lid closed for 15 minutes. 3. Oil the cooking grates, then place the salmon fillets on the grill grate. Cook, uncovered, for 2 to 3 minutes per side until the salmon turns bright pink. Remove from the heat and serve.

Spiced Sea Bass

Prep Time: 15 minutes | Cook Time: 6 minutes | Serves: 4

1 tablespoon paprika
2 teaspoons ground cumin
1 teaspoon ground coriander
1 teaspoon ground turmeric
1 teaspoon garam masala

½ teaspoon cayenne pepper
½ teaspoon black pepper
½ teaspoon salt
1 tablespoon olive oil
4 (6- to 8-ounce) sea bass fillets, skinned

1. In a small bowl, stir together the paprika, cumin, coriander, turmeric, garam masala, cayenne, black pepper, and salt until blended. Brush olive oil on all sides of the sea bass fillets. Sprinkle a generous amount of rub on the fillets until well coated on both sides. Cover with plastic wrap and refrigerate for 20 minutes. 2. R Set Traeger temperature to 425°F and preheat, lid closed for 15 minutes. 3. Oil the cooking grates, then place the sea bass on the grill grate. Cook, uncovered, for 3 to 4 minutes per side until the fish is firm to the touch. 4. Remove from the heat and serve immediately.

Halibut with Tomato-Herb Sauce

Prep Time: 15 minutes | Cook Time: 6 minutes | Serves: 4

½ cup olive oil
4 Roma tomatoes, diced
¼ cup chopped fresh basil leaves
¼ cup chopped fresh parsley

2 tablespoons freshly squeezed lemon juice
½ teaspoon salt, plus more for seasoning
¼ teaspoon black pepper, plus more for seasoning
4 (6- to 8-ounce) halibut fillets

1. In a medium bowl, mix the olive oil, tomatoes, basil, parsley, lemon juice, salt, and pepper to combine. Cover and set aside at room temperature until serving. 2. Season each halibut fillet with a pinch of salt and pepper. 3. Set Traeger temperature to 425°F and preheat, lid closed for 15 minutes. 4. Oil the cooking grates, then place the halibut fillets on the grill grate. Cook, uncovered, for 3 to 4 minutes per side until the fish is tender and white in color. 5. Top each halibut fillet with sauce and serve.

Savory Crab Cakes with Spicy Mayo

Prep Time: 20 minutes | Cook Time: 20 minutes | Serves: 4

3 tablespoons olive oil, divided
1 red bell pepper, seeded, stemmed, and diced
1 onion, diced
3 celery stalks, diced
Kosher salt
Freshly ground black pepper
Pinch red pepper flakes
3 garlic cloves, minced

2 tablespoons freshly squeezed lemon juice, divided
1½ tablespoons seafood seasoning, divided
1 pound cooked jumbo lump crabmeat
2 eggs, beaten
1 cup panko bread crumbs
1 cup mayonnaise
A few dashes hot sauce of choice
Lemon wedges, for serving (optional)

1. In a large skillet, heat 1 tablespoon of olive oil over medium-high heat. Once hot, add the bell pepper, onion, celery, and a pinch each of salt, black pepper, and red pepper flakes. Cook for 8 to 10 minutes, stirring occasionally. 2. Add the garlic, 1 tablespoon of lemon juice, and ½ tablespoon of seafood seasoning and cook for 1 minute more. Remove from the heat and set the mixture aside to cool. 3. Once the mixture has cooled, add the crabmeat, eggs, and bread crumbs. Gently mix this together and form eight patties with your hands. Place them on a tray or baking sheet and refrigerate for 1 hour. 4. When ready to make the crab cakes, place a cast-iron skillet on the grill grate, set Traeger temperature to 450°F and preheat, lid closed for 15 minutes. 5. Drizzle the remaining 2 tablespoons of olive oil into the skillet and place the crab cakes in it, being careful not to crowd them. 6. Flip the crab cakes after 10 minutes and cook for 10 minutes more. While the crab cakes cook, mix together the mayonnaise, hot sauce, remaining 1 tablespoon of lemon juice, and remaining 1 tablespoon of seafood seasoning. 7. Serve the crab cakes with the spicy mayo on the side and lemon wedges (if using).

Blackened Tilapia Tacos

Prep Time: 10 minutes | Cook Time: 10 minutes | Serves: 4

4 tilapia fillets
2 tablespoons blackened seasoning
Optional toppings: lettuce, salsa, pickled jalapeño peppers, guacamole, etc.

1 tablespoon olive oil
8-12 Tortillas of choice (flour or corn)

1. Place a cast-iron skillet or baking sheet on the grill grate, set Traeger temperature to 450°F and preheat, lid closed for 15 minutes. 2. Sprinkle both sides of the tilapia with the blackened seasoning. 3. Drizzle the olive oil into the skillet or baking sheet and place the tilapia fillets on top of the oil. Cook the tilapia for 4 to 5 minutes per side. Place the tortillas on the grill grates for a minute or two to warm them. 4. Remove the fish from the grill, flake it into smaller pieces, and assemble the tacos with your choice of toppings.

Bacon-Wrapped Scallops with Cilantro Butter

Prep Time: 45 minutes | Cook Time: 18 minutes | Serves: 6

8 tablespoons (1 stick) salted butter, softened
½ cup chopped fresh cilantro
1 jalapeño, finely diced
Juice of 1 lime, plus extra lime wedges for serving

10 to 12 large scallops, preferably diver scallops
1½ tablespoons Southwestern Seasoning
1 (12-ounce) package thin-cut bacon

1. In a bowl, combine the softened butter, cilantro, jalapeño, and lime juice and stir to combine thoroughly. Spoon the butter onto a piece of plastic wrap and form it into a log shape by rolling it in the plastic and sealing the ends. Refrigerate to firm it up before use. 2. Lay the scallops on a cutting board and pat them dry with paper towels. Sprinkle both sides with the seasoning and set them aside. 3. Cut the bacon strips in half lengthwise. Lay a scallop, flat-side down, in the middle of one half of a piece of bacon and fold the bacon over on both sides of the scallop. Cut the bacon with a knife or scissors until you have about ½ to 1 inch of overlap on the two ends. Flip the scallop over, rotate it 90 degrees, and lay it seam-side down on the other half piece of bacon, in a plus-sign shape. Fold the bacon over the scallop and cut it so you have a 1-inch overlap. Make sure the bacon is tight around the scallop. Repeat with the remaining scallops and bacon, place them seam-side down on a plate, cover, and refrigerate until ready to cook. 4. Set Traeger temperature to 300°F and preheat, lid closed for 15 minutes. 5. When the grill is ready, remove both the butter and scallops from the refrigerator. Slice the butter into the same number of disks as scallops and place one on top of each scallop. Open the grill lid and place each butter-topped scallop seam-side down on the grill grate. Close the lid and cook for 8 to 10 minutes. Open the lid and rotate the scallops 180 degrees, close the lid, and cook for another 8 to 10 minutes. Open the lid and check the internal temperature of the scallop with an instant-read thermometer. You are looking for an internal temperature of 125°F to 130°F and for the bacon to be cooked. 6. When the scallops are done, remove them from the grill and let rest for 5 to 10 minutes. Serve with lime wedges on the side.

Lemon Garlic Lobster Tail Skewers

Prep Time: 30 minutes | Cook Time: 10 minutes | Serves: 6

4 to 6 lobster tails
Juice of 1 lemon, divided
1¼ tablespoons Poultry and Seafood Rub
1 cup (2 sticks) salted butter, melted

5 or 6 garlic cloves, minced
4 to 6 thyme sprigs
Smoked Garlic Aioli, for serving
Lemon wedges, for serving

1. With a pair of kitchen shears, cut down the center back of each tail to open up the shell. Remove the meat in one piece and lay it out on a cutting board. Skewer each tail on a wood or metal skewer. (If using wooden skewers, soak them in water for 10 to 20 minutes so they don't burn while cooking.) Squeeze half the lemon juice over the skewers and season both sides with the rub. Place them in the refrigerator while you ready your grill. 2. Set Traeger temperature to 350°F and preheat, lid closed for 15 minutes. 3. In a small disposable aluminum loaf pan, combine the butter, the remaining lemon juice, the garlic, and thyme. Place the pan in the grill to warm through for 10 to 15 minutes, until the butter melts. Remove the skewers from the refrigerator and brush them with the melted butter. Place the skewers directly on the grill grate. Cook for 1 to 2 minutes, brush them with butter, then flip them over and brush again. Cook for another 1 to 2 minutes, brush them with butter, then flip again. Continue to flip and baste with butter until the internal temperature of the lobster is about 135°F. 4. The lobster tails are done when they turn white and are no longer gray. Remove them from the grill and baste them again with the butter. Let rest for 5 to 10 minutes. 5. Serve the skewers individually with aioli and lemon wedges on the side. Cheers!

Garlic Butter Crawfish Skewers

Prep Time: 20 minutes | Cook Time: 10 minutes | Serves: 6

2 large sweet onions, cut into bite-size pieces
2 to 3 pounds fresh raw crawfish tails, shelled
1 large green bell pepper, cut into bite-size pieces
1 large red bell pepper, cut into bite-size pieces
2 tablespoons Poultry and Seafood Rub
1 cup (2 sticks) salted butter, softened

1 shallot, diced
5 or 6 garlic cloves, minced
1 tablespoon cayenne pepper
1 tablespoon Old Bay Seasoning
Steamed rice, for serving

1. On a presoaked wood or metal skewer, thread a piece of onion, then a crawfish tail, then a green and red bell pepper piece, repeating the process until the skewer is full. Thread the remaining ingredients on skewers and refrigerate them all until you're ready to cook. 2. In a small disposable aluminum loaf pan, combine the rub, butter, shallot, garlic, cayenne, and Old Bay and blend them thoroughly. 3. Set Traeger temperature to 450°F and preheat, lid closed for 15 minutes. 4. When the grill is up to temperature, place the aluminum loaf pan on the grill, close the lid, and cook for 5 to 10 minutes, until the butter is melted, then move it to the side of the grill. Then place the skewers evenly around the grill and brush them with the butter. Close the lid and cook for 1 to 2 minutes. Open the lid, brush the skewers with more butter, and give them a flip. Brush again with butter and cook for another 1 to 2 minutes, leaving the grill lid open. Baste the tails with butter throughout the cook time. When the crawfish tails are no longer gray but a pinkish-red color, they are done. 5. Remove the skewers and let rest on a plate for 5 to 10 minutes. 6. To serve, place the skewers over a bed of rice and drizzle any reserved butter over them.

Maple-Walnut Crusted Salmon

Prep Time: 20 minutes | Cook Time: 30 minutes | Serves: 4

4 (8-ounce) salmon fillets, trimmed, skin removed, and checked for bones
Flaked sea salt
Freshly ground black pepper

Grated zest of 2 lemons, plus juice of 2 lemons, plus 1 lemon, quartered, for serving
1 cup walnuts, finely chopped
1 cup pure maple syrup

1. Set Traeger temperature to 275°F and preheat, lid closed for 15 minutes. 2. Season the salmon fillets on both sides with salt and pepper. Top each with lemon zest. 3. On a piece of parchment paper, arrange the chopped walnuts. 4. Brush each fillet with maple syrup and press the fillets into the walnuts. Place the fillets on a maple plank. Drizzle with lemon juice. Place the plank on the grill grate. Cook for 20 to 30 minutes, until the salmon is lightly browned and crispy. 5. Serve with lemon wedges for squeezing.

Marinated Mahimahi with Bang Bang Sauce

Prep Time: 10 minutes | Cook Time: 15 minutes | Serves: 4

4 mahimahi fillets
¼ cup soy sauce
1 tablespoon olive oil
1 tablespoon ginger paste

½ tablespoon garlic paste
½ cup mayonnaise
½ cup sweet Thai chile sauce
2 tablespoons sriracha

1. Place the mahimahi fillets in a gallon-size plastic bag. In a small bowl, whisk together the soy sauce, olive oil, ginger paste, and garlic paste until combined, then add the sauce to the bag with the mahimahi. Massage the bag until the fish is coated. Marinate for 1 hour in the refrigerator. 2. Set Traeger temperature to 400°F and preheat, lid closed for 15 minutes. 3. Put the fish on the grill grate and cook for 6 to 8 minutes per side. 4. While the fish cooks, make the bang bang sauce. In a small bowl, mix together the mayonnaise, chile sauce, and sriracha until combined. 5. Serve the mahimahi with the bang bang sauce on the side.

Tuna Sliders with Wasabi Broccoli Slaw

Prep Time: 2 hours | Cook Time: 15 minutes | Serves: 6

8 to 12 (1½-inch-thick) sushi-grade ahi tuna steaks
½ cup soy sauce
¼ cup ponzu
1 tablespoon sriracha
1 teaspoon toasted sesame oil
1 teaspoon ground ginger or grated fresh ginger

1 (16-ounce) bag shredded broccoli
½ cup mayonnaise
1½ teaspoons wasabi paste, plus more to taste
1 (12-pack) sesame seed slider buns
Avocado oil spray

1. Cut the tuna steaks down to roughly the size of the slider buns and pat them dry with a paper towel. 2. In a glass bowl, combine the soy sauce, ponzu, sriracha, sesame oil, and ginger. Add the tuna steaks to the marinade, mix to cover thoroughly, and refrigerate for 2 to 3 hours. 3. In a bowl, combine the shredded broccoli, mayonnaise, and wasabi paste. Taste and add more wasabi paste if you like more kick. Cover and refrigerate until ready to serve. 4. Set Traeger temperature to 450°F and preheat, lid closed for 15 minutes. 5. Remove the tuna steaks from the marinade and discard any excess marinade. Spray the grates with avocado oil, then place the tuna on the grill grates. Close the lid and cook for 1 minute. Flip and cook for 1 minute. Then, spray the steaks with avocado oil, and carefully flip them. Close the lid and cook for 1 minute more. Open the lid and, using an instant-read thermometer, test the internal temperature. I like mine medium-rare to medium, or an internal temperature of 120°F to 125°F. 6. When the steaks are to your desired doneness, remove them from the grill and let rest for 5 minutes. While the steaks are resting, toast the slider buns on the grill grate for a minute or two until they get a nice char on the inside but are not burnt. 7. To serve, place a tuna steak on the bottom bun, top it with a spoonful of broccoli slaw, add the top bun, and dig in!

Seared Scallops and Cheese Grits

Prep Time: 30 minutes | Cook Time: 6 minutes | Serves: 4

7 tablespoons unsalted butter, divided
⅓ cup panko bread crumbs
1 garlic clove, minced or pushed through a press
Grits:
3 ½ cups whole milk, plus more if needed
2 garlic cloves, minced or pushed through a press
¾ cup quick-cooking grits
4 ounces grated extra-sharp white cheddar cheese
Freshly ground black pepper

2 teaspoons finely chopped fresh thyme leaves
Kosher salt

16 sea scallops, each about 2 ounces
1¼ teaspoons Cajun seasoning
4 scallions, ends trimmed
Hot pepper sauce
1 tablespoon finely chopped fresh Italian parsley leaves

1. In a skillet over medium heat, melt the butter. Pour 5 tablespoons of the butter into a bowl; set aside. Add the panko and the garlic to the remaining 2 tablespoons butter in the skillet and cook until the panko is crisp and golden, 3 to 4 minutes, stirring often. Stir in the thyme and ⅛ teaspoon salt. Remove from the heat. 2. Set Traeger temperature to 500°F and preheat, lid closed for 15 minutes. 3. In a saucepan combine 3½ cups milk, the garlic, and ¾ teaspoon salt. Bring to a simmer over medium-high heat. Gradually whisk in the grits. Reduce the heat to low and continue cooking until the mixture thickens and the grits are very tender, 6 to 9 minutes, whisking often and adding water ¼ cup at a time if the mixture seems too thick. Stir in the cheese and season with pepper. Remove from the heat and cover to keep warm. 4. Pat the scallops dry. Remove and discard the small, tough side muscle that might be left on each one. In a bowl combine the scallops, Cajun seasoning, ½ teaspoon salt, and ¼ teaspoon pepper. Turn the scallops in the seasonings, and then add 2 tablespoons of the melted butter and toss to coat. 5. Grill the scallops, with the lid closed, until they are lightly browned and just opaque in the center, 4 to 6 minutes, turning twice. Transfer the scallops to a clean bowl. Add the remaining 3 tablespoons melted butter and 1 tablespoon hot pepper sauce, to taste; toss to coat. Roughly chop the scallions. 6. If the grits have solidified, loosen them with a few tablespoons of water or milk and warm through. Divide the grits among four plates. Top each serving with scallions, scallops, and bread crumbs. Garnish with parsley and serve immediately with additional hot pepper sauce, if desired.

Shrimp-Zucchini Kabobs with Pistachio-Tarragon Pesto

Prep Time: 50 minutes | Cook Time: 5 minutes | Serves: 4

¾ cup roughly chopped fresh Italian parsley leaves
¼ cup roughly chopped fresh tarragon leaves
¼ cup shelled unsalted pistachios
5 teaspoons fresh lemon juice
1 garlic clove, peeled and smashed
Kosher salt
Freshly ground black pepper
Extra-virgin olive oil

1 tablespoon water
32 large shrimp (21/30 count), peeled and deveined, tails left on
24 grape tomatoes
2 small zucchinis, each halved lengthwise and cut crosswise into 24 half-moons
1 large yellow bell pepper, cut into 24 pieces
12 scallions (white and light green parts only), cut into 24 pieces
Lemon wedges

1. If using bamboo skewers, soak in water for at least 30 minutes. 2. In a food processor, combine the parsley, tarragon, pistachios, lemon juice, garlic, ¼ teaspoon salt, and ¼ teaspoon pepper. Process until the mixture is finely ground, 30 seconds to 1 minute. With the motor running, slowly pour ½ cup oil through the feed tube and process until smooth, scraping down the sides of the bowl once or twice. Transfer ⅓ cup of the pesto to a bowl for brushing on the kabobs. Transfer the remaining pesto to another bowl and stir in the water to loosen the pesto slightly. Set aside for serving. 3. Set Traeger temperature to 500°F and preheat, lid closed for 15 minutes. 4. Thread the shrimp, tomatoes, zucchini, bell pepper, and scallions alternately onto skewers. Brush the ingredients with oil, and then brush them evenly with the reserved ⅓ cup pesto. Lightly season with salt and pepper. Grill the kabobs, with the lid closed, until the shrimp are just firm to the touch and opaque in the center, 3 to 5 minutes, turning once or twice. The vegetables will be crisp-tender. Remove from the grill. Drizzle the remaining pesto over the kabobs and squeeze the lemon on top.

Lemon Cheese Risotto with Grilled Asparagus & Shrimp

Prep Time: 20 minutes | Cook Time: 30 minutes | Serves: 8

1-pound asparagus
Extra-virgin olive oil
Kosher salt
Risotto:
6 cups low-sodium chicken broth
3 tablespoons unsalted butter, divided
2 tablespoons extra-virgin olive oil
½ cup finely chopped yellow onion
1 teaspoon kosher salt, divided
2 cups arborio rice
½ cup dry white wine

18 extra-large shrimp (16/20 count), peeled and deveined, tails removed
1 tablespoon fresh lemon juice

½ cup finely grated Parmigiano-Reggiano® cheese, divided
1 tablespoon finely grated lemon zest
¼ cup fresh lemon juice
2 tablespoons finely chopped fresh Italian parsley leaves
1 tablespoon finely chopped fresh mint leaves
Freshly ground black pepper

1. Set Traeger temperature to 400°F and preheat, lid closed for 15 minutes. 2. Remove and discard the tough bottom of each asparagus spear by grasping each end and bending it gently until it snaps at its natural point of tenderness, usually about two-thirds of the way down the spear. Place the asparagus on a plate and drizzle with oil, turning to coat. Season with salt. 3. Brush the shrimp with oil and lightly season with salt. 4. Grill the asparagus (perpendicular to the bars on the cooking grate), with the lid closed, until browned in spots and crisp-tender, 6 to 8 minutes, turning occasionally. At the same time, grill the shrimp until slightly firm on the surface and opaque in the center, 3 to 5 minutes, turning once. Remove from the grill as they are done. Toss the shrimp with the lemon juice. When the asparagus and shrimp are cool enough to handle, cut them into 1-inch pieces. Set aside. 5. In a medium saucepan over high heat, bring the broth to a simmer. Keep warm. 6. In a large saucepan over medium heat, melt 2 tablespoons of the butter with the oil. Add the onion and ½ teaspoon of the salt. Sauté until the onion is softened but not browned, 3 to 4 minutes. Add the rice and cook until the grains are coated with the butter mixture and turn opaque, about 2 minutes, stirring frequently. Add the wine and stir until evaporated, about 1 minute. Add 1 cup of the warm broth. Simmer until the rice has absorbed nearly all of the liquid, stirring occasionally. Add the remaining broth ½ cup at a time, stirring until nearly all of the liquid is absorbed before adding the next addition, 25 to 30 minutes in all. At this point the risotto should be creamy and the grains should be plump and tender, yet firm to the bite. 7. Remove the risotto from the heat and stir in the remaining 1 tablespoon butter, ¼ cup of the cheese, the lemon zest and juice, and the remaining ½ teaspoon salt. Fold in the asparagus, shrimp, parsley, and mint and season with pepper. Divide the risotto among serving bowls, garnish with the remaining ¼ cup cheese, and serve immediately.

Crunchy Shrimp and Scallop Skewers

Prep Time: 15 minutes | Cook Time: 6 minutes | Serves: 4

Breading:

1 cup fresh bread crumbs

1 tablespoon finely chopped fresh Italian parsley leaves

1 teaspoon dried oregano

½ teaspoon smoked paprika

½ teaspoon freshly ground black pepper

1 medium garlic clove, minced or pushed through a press

¼ teaspoon kosher salt

Extra-virgin olive oil

12 large shrimp (21/30 count), peeled and deveined, tails removed

12 sea scallops, each 1–1½ ounces

1 lemon, cut into wedges

1. If using bamboo skewers, soak in water for at least 30 minutes. 2. Set Traeger temperature to 500°F and preheat, lid closed for 15 minutes. 3. In a shallow dish combine the breading ingredients, including 1 tablespoon oil. 4. Pat dry the scallops. Remove and discard the small, tough side muscle that might be left on each scallop. Thread the shrimp and scallops on their own skewers. Lightly brush the shellfish on both sides with oil and then press them into the breading mixture to coat, patting the crumbs firmly to help them adhere. Let stand for 5 minutes to allow the breading to set. 5. Grill the skewers, with the lid closed, until the shellfish is just opaque in the center and the crumbs are golden brown, turning once or twice (some of the crumbs may become slightly charred). The scallops will take about 6 minutes, and the shrimp will take about 4 minutes. 6. Remove from the grill and serve immediately with the lemon wedges.

Grilled Shrimp, Corn and Avocado Salad

Prep Time: 30 minutes | Cook Time: 15 minutes | Serves: 6

1 ear of corn, husk and silk removed

Avocado oil spray

1½ tablespoons Poultry and Seafood Rub

18 large raw shrimp, peeled and deveined

3 avocados

¼ cup diced red onion

1 Roma tomato, cored, seeded, and diced

1 jalapeño, diced

2 cups shredded green cabbage

¼ cup chopped fresh cilantro, plus extra for garnish

2 limes

Salt

Freshly ground black pepper

½ teaspoon toasted sesame oil

1. Set Traeger temperature to 350°F and preheat, lid closed for 15 minutes. 2. Spray the ear of corn with avocado oil and lightly sprinkle it with the rub. When the grill is ready, place the corn on the grill and cook, rotating it occasionally, for 8 to 10 minutes, until the corn has caramelized and turned golden brown. Remove the corn and set aside. 3. Skewer 4 or 5 shrimp on a wooden skewer, leaving space between each shrimp. Sprinkle both sides with the rub and spray with avocado oil. Repeat with the remaining shrimp, then place the skewers on the grill grate and cook for 1 to 2 minutes per side; the shrimp are done when they turn pink. Remove the shrimp from the grill and set aside. 4. Halve the avocados and remove the pits. Scoop out the avocado into a bowl, reserving the empty skins. Mash the avocado with a fork into a smooth yet chunky texture. Add the onion, tomatoes, jalapeños, cabbage, and cilantro, then stir to combine. 5. Slice the corn kernels off the cob and add them to the avocado mixture, squeeze the juice of 1 lime into the mixture, and season with salt and pepper to taste. Drizzle the sesame oil over the mixture and stir to combine. 6. Divide the avocado mixture evenly among the avocado shell halves and top each with 3 shrimp. Garnish with cilantro and cut the remaining lime into wedges for serving.

Easy Grilled Salmon

Prep Time: 5 minutes | Cook Time: 20 minutes | Serves: 4

1 (2-pound) half salmon fillet, skin-on

Superb Seafood Rub

1. Set Traeger temperature to 350°F and preheat, lid closed for 15 minutes. 2. Sprinkle the salmon with the rub to taste. 3. Place the salmon on the grill grate, skin-side down. Close the lid and grill for about 20 minutes, or until the internal temperature reaches 145°F. 4. Remove the salmon from the grill and serve immediately.

Grilled Lobster Tails with Tarragon Butter

Prep Time: 15 minutes | Cook Time: 10 minutes | Serves: 4

½ cup (1 stick) unsalted butter
2 cloves garlic, finely chopped
1 tablespoon finely chopped shallot
1 tablespoon chopped fresh tarragon
Grated zest of 1 lemon

Kosher salt
8 (8-inch) metal skewers
8 lobster tails (4 ounces each)
Truffle oil for drizzling (optional)

1. Set Traeger temperature to 400°F and preheat, lid closed for 15 minutes. 2. Meanwhile, in a small saucepan over low heat, melt the butter, then stir in the garlic, shallot, tarragon, and lemon zest and let simmer for a few minutes, until fragrant. Salt to taste. Remove from the heat. 3. Run skewers down the length of each lobster tail. This will help them lie flat on the grill. Place them on the grill, meat side down, close the lid, and cook for about 3 minutes. Turn them over, spoon some of the tarragon butter over each, close the lid, and cook until the meat firms up, another 4 to 5 minutes. Check by pressing on the front part of the tail where the meat is exposed. 4. Remove from the heat, remove the skewers, crack the tails, spoon some more of the butter over each tail, drizzle with truffle oil if using, and serve.

Cheese-Spinach Stuffed Salmon

Prep Time: 10 minutes | Cook Time: 13 minutes | Serves: 8

10 ounces fresh spinach leaves, well washed and trimmed of heavy stems
4 ounces herb-flavored goat cheese, at room temperature
Pinch of freshly grated nutmeg
Kosher salt and freshly ground black pepper

1 (4-pound) side of salmon
Olive oil for brushing
2 cups plain dry breadcrumbs
½ cup (1 stick) unsalted butter, melted

1. Blanch the spinach in a pot of boiling salted water until wilted, which should take about 30 seconds. Drain and rinse with cold water. Roll the spinach up in paper towels and squeeze to get out as much water out as possible. Finely chop the spinach and put in a bowl. Add the goat cheese, nutmeg, salt, and pepper and stir until well combined. 2. Cut a ½-inch-deep pocket along the top of the salmon, running its entire length. Use your fingers to open the pocket and stuff as much of the spinach mixture into the pocket as possible. Mound the rest on top of the salmon. Brush a rimmed baking sheet with olive oil. Place the salmon on the baking sheet. 3. Set Traeger temperature to 400°F and preheat, lid closed for 15 minutes. 4. Toss the breadcrumbs and melted butter together and sprinkle over the top of the salmon to form a crust. Place the baking pan on the grill and close the lid. Roast until the tip of a cake tester stuck into the thickest part of the salmon is just warm when touched to your lip, about 12 minutes. 5. Remove the pan from the grill and, using two long spatulas, transfer the salmon to a platter, and serve.

Grilled Salmon with Tarragon

Prep Time: 20 minutes | Cook Time: 20-30 minutes | Serves: 4

¼ cup mayonnaise
2 tablespoons stone-ground mustard
2 tarragon sprigs, leaves stripped and finely sliced, plus more for garnish
Grated zest of 1 lemon, plus juice of 1 lemon, plus 1 lemon,

quartered, for serving
4 (8-ounce) salmon fillets, skin removed and deboned
Flaked sea salt
Freshly ground black pepper

1. Set Traeger temperature to 275°F and preheat, lid closed for 15 minutes. 2. In a large bowl, whisk together the mayonnaise, mustard, tarragon, lemon zest, and half the lemon juice. 3. Season the salmon on both sides with salt and pepper. Top each fillet with the mayonnaise mixture. 4. Place the fillets on the grill grate, leaving space between each one. Drizzle with the remaining lemon juice. Grill for 20 to 30 minutes, until lightly browned. Total grilling time will depend on your desired doneness and the thickness of the fillets. Test for doneness by sliding a paring knife into the thickest part of a fillet and leaving it there for 5 seconds. Remove the knife and gently touch the flat side to your lower lip—if the knife is warm, the salmon is fully cooked. 5. Top with a sprinkle of tarragon. Serve with lemon wedges for squeezing.

Seafood Stew with Garlic Croutons

Prep Time: 40 minutes | Cook Time: 45 minutes | Serves: 6

Extra-virgin olive oil
1 cup finely chopped yellow onion
1 medium fennel bulb, cored and thinly sliced
3 garlic cloves, smashed
1 small red bell pepper, cut into ¼-inch dice
1 teaspoon dried oregano
¼ teaspoon crushed red pepper flakes
1 can (28 ounces) Italian plum tomatoes in juice
4 cups low-sodium chicken broth
1 tablespoon tomato paste
1 bay leaf

Kosher salt
Freshly ground black pepper
24 large shrimp (2⅕0 count), peeled and deveined, tails left on
12 large sea scallops, each about 1 ½ ounces
1 large garlic clove, finely grated, minced, or pushed through a press
½ loaf ciabatta or other Italian bread, cut into 1 ½ inch cubes (12–16 pieces)
24 live mussels, about 1-pound total, scrubbed and debearded
¼ cup finely chopped fresh Italian parsley leaves

1. In a large pot over medium heat, warm 2 tablespoons oil. Add the onion and the fennel and sauté until the vegetables begin to soften, about 5 minutes. Add the smashed garlic, bell pepper, oregano, and red pepper flakes and sauté for 2 minutes. Add the tomatoes and their juice (crushing the tomatoes with your hands before adding them to the pot), the broth, tomato paste, bay leaf, 1 teaspoon salt, and ¼ teaspoon pepper. Bring to a boil, reduce the heat to medium-low, and simmer, partially covered, for 30 minutes, stirring occasionally. 2. Set Traeger temperature to 500°F and preheat, lid closed for 15 minutes. 3. Rinse the shrimp and the scallops under cold water and pat dry. Remove the small, tough side muscle that might be left on each scallop. Brush the shellfish on all sides with oil and lightly season with salt and pepper. 4. Combine 2 tablespoons oil, the finely grated garlic, and the bread cubes and toss to coat. 5. Grill the shrimp and the scallops, with the lid closed, until they are just opaque in the center, turning once. The shrimp will take 2 to 4 minutes and the scallops will take 4 to 6 minutes. Remove from the grill as they are done. 6. Lower the temperature of the grill to 400°F. Grill the bread cubes, with the lid closed, until lightly browned on all sides, about 4 minutes, turning several times. 7. Just before serving, return the stew to a vigorous simmer over medium heat. Add the mussels, cover the pot, and cook until the mussels open, 3 to 5 minutes (discard any unopened mussels). Stir in the scallops and shrimp. Ladle the stew into wide soup bowls. Top with the parsley, garnish with the croutons, and serve warm.

Hearty Shrimp, Chicken, and Sausage Paella

Prep Time: 20 minutes | Cook Time: 1 hour | Serves: 8

6 bone-in, skin-on chicken thighs
1 linguica sausage
1-pound bulk (raw) chorizo sausage
½ cup chopped red onion
½ cup chopped green bell pepper
¼ cup prepared sofrito (available in the Hispanic section of the supermarket)
1 cup long-grain rice
4 cups low-sodium chicken broth, divided
1 tablespoon chopped fresh thyme

1 teaspoon turmeric
½ teaspoon smoked paprika
½ teaspoon saffron threads, crushed between your fingers
2 cloves garlic, finely minced
1 pound 34/40-count shrimp, shells left on, cut down the back and veins removed (cooking the shrimp with their shells will add a ton of flavor to the paella)
½ cup green peas
1 tablespoon chopped fresh oregano

1. Set Traeger temperature to 450°F and preheat, lid closed for 15 minutes. 2. Place the chicken thighs and linguica sausage on the grill; sear the chicken about 5 minutes per side and cook the sausage, turning, for about 5 minutes. Remove the chicken and sausage to a plate. 3. Place a 15-inch cast-iron skillet on the grill. Give it a few minutes to heat up, then add the chorizo. Cook it until browned, crisp, and cooked all the way through, breaking it up with a wooden spoon. Using a slotted spoon, remove the sausage from the pan to the plate. Add the onion and bell pepper to the rendered fat in the pan and cook until softened, about 5 minutes, stirring a few times. Add the sofrito and cook, stirring, for about 2 minutes. Stir in the rice and let toast 2 to 3 minutes. Pour in 2 cups of broth and bring to a boil. Close the lid and cook for 10 minutes. 4. Add the thyme, turmeric, paprika, saffron, and garlic. Stir to work into the rice. 5. Slice the linguica across on an angle into 8 pieces. Add the chicken, sliced sausage, and chorizo to the pan along with another 1 cup of broth and stir, then close the lid. 6. After 20 minutes, stir in the shrimp and peas. If the rice is looking dry, add the remaining cup of broth. Close the lid and cook until the shrimp are done, another 7 to 10 minutes. 7. Remove the pan from the grill and sprinkle with the oregano. Serve immediately.

BBQ Lemon Trout

Prep Time: 5 minutes | Cook Time: 25 minutes | Serves: 4

2 (1-pound) trout fillets, butterflied
Superb Seafood Rub

1 lemon, sliced into rounds

1. Set Traeger temperature to 325°F and preheat, lid closed for 15 minutes. 2. Sprinkle the inside of the trout fillets with the seafood rub to taste. 3. Place the lemon slices inside the trout fillets. 4. Set the trout on the grill grate, close the lid, and grill for about 25 minutes, or until the internal temperature reaches 145°F. 5. Remove the trout from the grill and serve immediately.

Teriyaki Shrimp-Pineapple Skewers

Prep Time: 20 minutes | Cook Time: 30 minutes | Serves: 4

24 large raw shrimp (21 to 25 per pound), thawed if frozen, peeled, and deveined
1 pineapple, trimmed, peeled, quartered lengthwise, cored, and cut into large dice
4 cilantro sprigs, leaves stripped and finely sliced, plus more for garnish
4 garlic cloves, minced
4 scallions, trimmed and finely sliced on a 45-degree angle

¼ cup soy sauce
2 tablespoons fish sauce
Grated zest of 2 limes, plus juice of 2 limes
2 tablespoons dark brown sugar
1 tablespoon finely grated fresh ginger
1 teaspoon sesame oil
Flaked sea salt
Freshly ground black pepper

1. Alternate 3 shrimp with 3 pineapple chunks on each of 8 bamboo skewers that have been soaked in water. 2. In a large bowl, whisk together the cilantro, garlic, scallions, soy sauce, fish sauce, lime zest, lime juice, sugar, ginger, and sesame oil. Transfer to a large food-grade plastic bag and add the skewers. Remove as much air as possible from the bag and seal it. Refrigerate for 4 hours, turning the bag 2 or 3 times. 3. Remove the skewers, reserving the marinade in the refrigerator. 4. Set Traeger temperature to 275°F and preheat, lid closed for 15 minutes. 5. Place the skewers on the grill grate, leaving space between each one. Season with salt and pepper. Grill for 10 minutes. Brush the shrimp and pineapple with the reserved marinade. 6. Grill for about 20 minutes more, until the shrimp are fully cooked, pink, and firm.

Conclusion

In wrapping up this comprehensive guide to the Traeger Wood Fire Pellet Grill, it's clear that this versatile and powerful appliance is a game-changer for both novice and experienced grill enthusiasts. Throughout this cookbook, we've explored a myriad of recipes that showcase the grill's ability to grill, smoke, roast, bake, braise, and BBQ with ease, all while infusing your dishes with that signature wood-fired flavor.

The Traeger grill's ability to maintain consistent temperatures, its ease of use, and the enhanced flavors it imparts to food make it a standout choice for any cooking enthusiast. Whether you're preparing a weeknight dinner or hosting a large backyard barbecue, the Traeger grill proves to be an invaluable tool. Its user-friendly design, coupled with the ability to control and monitor cooking through the Traeger app, makes the cooking process not only efficient but also enjoyable.

We've also covered the essential tips and tricks to maximize your grilling experience, from selecting the right type of wood pellets to maintaining your grill in top condition. Proper care and maintenance ensure that your grill continues to perform at its best, providing you with delicious meals and reliable service for years to come.

This cookbook has been designed to provide you with not only recipes but also the knowledge and confidence to experiment and create your own culinary masterpieces. The versatility of the Traeger Wood Fire Pellet Grill enables you to explore a wide range of cooking techniques and flavors, making it an essential part of your kitchen arsenal.

As you continue your grilling journey, remember that the key to great cooking lies in enjoying the process and experimenting with different flavors and techniques. The Traeger Wood Fire Pellet Grill is designed to make this journey as enjoyable and rewarding as possible. Happy grilling, and may your culinary adventures be filled with delicious discoveries and unforgettable meals.

Appendix 1 Measurement Conversion Chart

VOLUME EQUIVALENTS (LIQUID)

US STANDARD	US STANDARD (OUNCES)	METRIC (APPROXIMATE)
2 tablespoons	1 fl.oz	30 mL
¼ cup	2 fl.oz	60 mL
½ cup	4 fl.oz	120 mL
1 cup	8 fl.oz	240 mL
1½ cup	12 fl.oz	355 mL
2 cups or 1 pint	16 fl.oz	475 mL
4 cups or 1 quart	32 fl.oz	1 L
1 gallon	128 fl.oz	4 L

VOLUME EQUIVALENTS (DRY)

US STANDARD	METRIC (APPROXIMATE)
⅛ teaspoon	0.5 mL
¼ teaspoon	1 mL
½ teaspoon	2 mL
¾ teaspoon	4 mL
1 teaspoon	5 mL
1 tablespoon	15 mL
¼ cup	59 mL
½ cup	118 mL
¾ cup	177 mL
1 cup	235 mL
2 cups	475 mL
3 cups	700 mL
4 cups	1 L

TEMPERATURES EQUIVALENTS

FAHRENHEIT(F)	CELSIUS(C) (APPROXIMATE)
225 °F	107 °C
250 °F	120 °C
275 °F	135 °C
300 °F	150 °C
325 °F	160 °C
350 °F	180 °C
375 °F	190 °C
400 °F	205 °C
425 °F	220 °C
450 °F	235 °C
475 °F	245 °C
500 °F	260 °C

WEIGHT EQUIVALENTS

US STANDARD	METRIC (APPROXINATE)
1 ounce	28 g
2 ounces	57 g
5 ounces	142 g
10 ounces	284 g
15 ounces	425 g
16 ounces (1 pound)	455 g
1.5 pounds	680 g
2 pounds	907 g

Appendix 2 Recipes Index

A

Apple-Cabbage Slaw 27
Aromatic Baby Back Ribs 63
Aromatic Braised Lamb 77
Aromatic Leg of Lamb with Roasted Potatoes 80
Asian-Inspired Coleslaw 25
Asian-Spiced Bok Choy 24
Authentic Chicken Marbella 37

B

Bacon and Butternut Squash Bread Pudding 18
Bacon and Mushroom Beef Burgers 50
Bacon-Wrapped Sausage Fatty 65
Bacon-Wrapped Scallops with Cilantro Butter 87
Ballistic BBQ Smoked Fryer Chicken 38
Balsamic Brussels Sprouts with Pomegranate Seeds,
Walnuts, and Grapes 22
Balsamic Portabello Mushroom & Cheese Panini 24
Balsamic Turnip Wedges with Goat Cheese 32
Barbecue Pork Riblets 65
Barbecue Pulled Beef 58
Barbecued Chicken Legs 44
Barbecued Rack of Lambs 78
Basil Marinated Lamb Rib Chops 81
BBQ Beef Brisket 51
BBQ Lemon Trout 94
BBQ Pulled Pork 71
BBQ Turkey Breast 36
Beef-Bacon Cheeseburgers 52
Beer and Cheese Bread 19
Beer Slow-Cooked Pinto Beans 26
Biscuit Breakfast Sausage Pudding 16
Blackened Tilapia Tacos 87
Brined Bone-In Pork Loin 66
Buffalo Cauliflower Steaks 32

C

California French Beef Roast 59
Caramelizd Beef Slices 60
Cedar Plank Grilled Salmon 84
Cedar-Plank Grilled Salmon 84
Charred Asparagus with Basil-Lime Sauce 28
Cheese Asparagus and Tomato Frittata 20
Cheese Corn and Pepper Salad 29
Cheese Pepperoni Mushroom Pizza 68
Cheese Potatoes 31
Cheese-Spinach Stuffed Salmon 92
Cheesy Biscuit and Gravy Breakfast Bake 16
Chicken Tagine with Tomato-Honey Jam 38
Chimichurri Beef 51
Citrus Pork Butt 72
Classic Beef Hamburgers 52
Classic Shakshouka 18
Cornbread 17
Cream Cheese Zucchini Baguette Sandwiches 14
Creole Chicken Breasts with Black-eyed Peas Salad 39

Crispy Potato Wedges 22
Crispy Sweet Potato Wedges 30
Crunchy Chicken 42
Crunchy Shrimp and Scallop Skewers 91
Cumin Lamb Kebabs 82
Curried Lamb Chops with Garlic-Yogurt Sauce 81

D

Delicious Barbecue Beef Back Ribs 57
Delicious Naan 19
Delicious Salmon Candy 85
Deviled Eggs 14
Dijon Thyme Grilled Rack of Lamb 79
Duck Jerky 44

E

Easy Grilled Salmon 91
Easy Smoked Turkey 37
Eggplant Cucumber Salad 23
Eggplant Slices with Spicy Dressing 31

F

Feta Lamb Burgers 76
Flavorful Pepper Steak Stir-Fry 58
Flavorful Roasted Suckling Pig 71
Fluffy Corn Bread 18
Fresh Huevos Rancheros 69

G

Garlic Beef Tenderloin with Romesco Sauce 59
Garlic Bok Choy with Sesame Seeds 27
Garlic Bread with Sun-Dried Tomatoes 14
Garlic Butter Crawfish Skewers 88
Garlic Leek and White Beans Casserole 23
Garlic New York Strip Roast 60
Garlic Prime Rib 57
Garlic T-Bone Steak with Blue Cheese Butter 56
Garlic-Sage Turkey Cutlets with Cranberry-Apple
Sauce 46
Garlic-Thyme Prime Rib Roast 52
Garlicky Prime Rib Roast 50
Greek Pork Souvlaki 70
Grilled Beets with Goat Cheese, Arugula, and
Pistachios 26
Grilled Butter Carrots 31
Grilled Cajun Mahi-Mahi 84
Grilled Chicken Breasts 37
Grilled Chicken Drumsticks and Peaches 47
Grilled Chicken Tenders 38
Grilled Corn on the Cob 25
Grilled Eggplant with Sun-Dried Tomato Vinaigrette 27
Grilled Flank Steak with Chimichurri 50
Grilled Hot Dogs with Spicy Pickled Vegetables 61
Grilled Italian-Style Portabellas 25
Grilled Lobster Tails with Tarragon Butter 92
Grilled Meat Loaf 56
Grilled Oysters with Lemon-Garlic Sauce 85
Grilled Pancetta-Wrapped Asparagus 32

Grilled Romaine Hearts Caesar Salad 30
Grilled Salmon with Tarragon 92
Grilled Sausage Olive Pizzas 66
Grilled Shrimp, Corn and Avocado Salad 91
Grilled T-Bone Steaks with Moroccan Spice Paste 61
Grilled Zucchini with Basil and Orange Zest 33

H

Halibut with Tomato-Herb Sauce 86
Hearty Shrimp, Chicken, and Sausage Paella 93
Herb-Butter Crusted Rack of Lamb 81
Herb-Garlic Leg of Lamb with Zucchini Salad 80
Herb-Garlic Rack of Lamb 79
Herb-Mustard Leg of Lamb 77
Herb-Smoked Whole Turkey 43
Herbed Ground Lamb Kebabs 75
Herbed Tri-Tip Sirloin 56
Homemade Pita Bread 17
Homemade Pork Belly Bacon 67
Honey-Lemon Glazed Chicken Thighs 46
Horseradish-Crusted Rib Roast with Butter Gravy 60

J

Jamaican Jerk Chicken Leg Quarters 41
Juicy Pork Chops 72
Juicy Venison Loin Roast 82

K

Korean-Inspired Short Ribs 59

L

Lamb and Cherry Tomato Kebabs 74
Lamb Cheeseburgers 78
Lamb Chops with Hot Pepper Jelly 79
Lemon Broccoli with Parmesan 24
Lemon Cheese Risotto with Grilled Asparagus & Shrimp 90
Lemon Garlic Lobster Tail Skewers 87
Lemon Pork Kebabs 64
Lemon-Honey Glazed Chicken Breasts 35
Lemon-Oregano Boneless Leg of Lamb 76
Lime Chicken with Aji Verde 39
Lime Spareribs with Adobo and Garlic Butter 70
Lime Tequila-Marinated Chicken Breasts with Cajun-Spiced Rice 41

M

Mango-Ginger Glazed Baby Back Ribs 67
Maple-Bourbon Pork Chops with Applesauce 67
Maple-Dijon Chicken 43
Maple-Walnut Crusted Salmon 88
Marinated Mahimahi with Bang Bang Sauce 88
Mexican Pork Loin Roast 65

N

No-Knead Bread 17

P

Pancetta Onion Frittata 16
Parmesan Meatballs 61
Pico De Gallo 26
Potato and Peas Frittata 15
Prosciutto Butter Grilled Chicken Thighs 43
Pulled Pork Stew 69

R

Rack of Lamb with Mint Sauce 82
Roast Beef, Potato and Egg Skillet 55

Rosemary Pork Loin Chops with Pear 64
Rosemary Roasted Chicken 45
Rosemary Veal Chops with Red Pepper-Butter Sauce 57
Rosemary-Garlic Leg of Lamb 75
Rosemary-Garlic Rack of Lamb 74

S

Salty and Sweet Turkey Legs 42
Savory Cauliflower Steaks 29
Savory Crab Cakes with Spicy Mayo 86
Savory Hoisin-Soy Lamb Shanks 76
Savory Jerk-Marinated Tofu 29
Savory Pork Sliders with Black Bean Salsa 68
Seafood Stew with Garlic Croutons 93
Seared Scallops and Cheese Grits 89
Shrimp-Zucchini Kabobs with Pistachio-Tarragon Pesto 90
Simple Smoked Spaghetti Squash 30
Skirt Steak Skewers with Green Chile Sauce 54
Smoked Beer Can Chicken 45
Smoked Chicken Breasts 41
Smoked Chicken Gumbo with Rice 35
Smoked Leg of Lamb with Fresh Mint Sauce 78
Southern Baked Beans 22
Spiced Chicken with Orange-Chipotle Barbecue Sauce 47
Spiced Citrus Duck with Plums 36
Spiced Rib Eyes Steaks 51
Spiced Salmon Fillets 85
Spiced Sea Bass 86
Spiced Whole Chicken 42
Spicy Beef Kabobs with Pineapple Salsa 54
Spicy Black Turtle Beans 23
Spicy Chicken Drumsticks 45
Spicy Lemongrass Chicken with Cilantro Pesto 40
Spicy Pork Sandwiches With Apple-Onion Chutney 63
Steak-Mushroom Kebabs with Yum Yum Sauce 53
Strawberry Pancake 15
Sweet & Spicy Tri-Tip Roast with Corn-Bean Salad 53
Sweet and Sour Short Ribs 55
Sweet and Spicy Cinnamon Turkey Wings 46
Sweet and Spicy Lamb Ribs 75
Sweet Country Sausage Baked Beans 15
Tea Smoked Whole Chicken 36

T

Teriyaki Chicken Skewers 48
Teriyaki Onion Pops 28
Teriyaki Pork Tenderloin 70
Teriyaki Shrimp-Pineapple Skewers 94
Texas Pork Steaks 64
Thyme Flank Steak with Balsamic Pearl Onions 58
Tuna Sliders with Wasabi Broccoli Slaw 89
Turkey Cutlets with Cherry–Cranberry Relish 40
Turkey Noodle Soup 44
Tuscan-Style Cannellini Beans 28

V

Venison Steaks with Blackberry Sauce 74
Vietnamese Pork Noodle 69

Made in United States
Troutdale, OR
09/02/2024

22539683R00063